1012 MONASTERY ROAD

D0838686

1012 Monastery Road

A Spiritual Journey

———◆◆———

WILLIAM MENINGER, OCSO

Lantern Books • New York
A Division of Booklight Inc.

2005
Lantern Books
One Union Square West, Suite 201
New York, NY 10003

Copyright William A. Meninger, OCSO, 2005, 1989

All rights reserved. No part of this book may be reproduced, stored in a
retrieval system or transmitted in any form or by any means, electronic,
mechanical, photocopying, recording or otherwise, without the written permission of Lantern Books.

Printed in the United States of America

All photos copyright John Ruzicka

Library of Congress Cataloging-in-Publication Data

Meninger, William.
1012 Monastery Road : a spiritual journey / William Meninger.—2nd ed.
p. cm.
ISBN 1-59056-063-9 (alk. paper)
1. Monastic and religious life. 2. St. Benedict's Monastery (Snowmass,
Colo.) 3. Trappists—Colorado—Snowmass—Spiritual life. I. Title: Ten
twelve Monastery Road. II. Title.
BX2435.M43 2005
255—dc22
2004028214

printed on 100% post-consumer waste paper, chlorine-free.

Dedicated to my mother,
Katherine T. Meninger

Acknowledgments

SCRIPTURE QUOTES ARE TAKEN FROM the *New English Bible*, Oxford University Press and Cambridge University Press, copyright 1961, 1970.

"Contemplative Prayer—Many Are Called," reprinted with permission of the editors of *Review for Religious*, St. Louis, MO.

Chap. 9 of this volume, "Beginning to Pray," taken from "Aspects of Prayer," *Word and Spirit*, vol. 3, 1981; "A Personal Christology," from *Word and Spirit*, vol. 4, 1982. Both articles reprinted with permission of St. Bede's Publications, Petersham, MA.

Quotes from *Our Town* by Thornton Wilder from Coward-McCann, Inc., New York.

Excerpts from *The Cloud of Unknowing* by William Johnston, copyright 1973 by William Johnston, reprinted by permission of Doubleday, a division of Bantam, Doubleday, Dell Publishing Group, Inc.

Contents

Preface to the Second Edition

WHY A NEW EDITION FOR a book about a form of monastic life that goes back for over 1,400 years? *1012 Monastery Road* was written in 1989. Does monasticism change so quickly that already a new edition is called for? The answer to that is yes and no. The roots of monasticism are intertwined with the roots of Christianity itself, and the fact that it has survived and flourished for so many centuries testifies to the veracity, stability, and permanence of its foundations.

Yet a short time ago in one of our weekly chapter meetings, the solemnly professed monks at 1012 Monastery Road met to discuss significant changes in our daily lives. Our community is aging. This is expected and inevitable. It calls for, among other things, a kind of infirmary for older monks. In addition, our horarium needs to be modified. To arise for the night office at 3:15 A.M. is increasingly difficult for our "ancients." Dietary changes to correspond with modern understanding of health needs must also be considered. At the same time the life must not be so weakened as to no longer present a challenge to the young. The Rule of St. Benedict, which establishes the ground rules for modern Cistercian living, is noted for its moderation—neither too ascetic for the elderly and inform nor too easygoing for the strong. So changes are inevitable and a good sign of growth, maturity and the establishment of a meaningful relationship with the modern world. Perhaps those lines from Alexander Pope are relevant here: Be not the first by whom the new is tried, nor yet the last to lay the old aside.

Balancing the needs of the day against the demands of monastic principles has been the duty of monks of the Benedictine Family since the seventh century. This has been done in many different ways. Regular yearly inspections by abbots of founding monasteries, periodic meetings of abbots in General Chapter embracing the whole Order, written reports to and by local bishops, and even observations by concerned neighbors have served these purposes.

Obviously, a rule written in the seventh century cannot be literally observed in the twenty-first. Thus, St. Benedict's mandate that the abbot must greet guests by washing their feet is better observed today by showing them the washroom. In order to keep the true spirit of the Rule, it must constantly be read and re-read in the light of the gospels and the signs of our times to discern meaningful and effective interpretations. In this way, it will continue to be a vibrant living and effective school of charity.

INTRODUCTION

IN MANY PARABLES, JESUS PRESENTS the Kingdom of God as a process of growth, both human and divine. Special environments are required for special kinds of growth. Contemplation is a sign of significant growth in the Kingdom of God. The proper environment for developing contemplation is a Christian community gathered together to listen to the word of God. Contemplation is the deepest level of listening to the word of God. The parish community is the gathering of the faithful in a particular geographical location to hear the word of God, to share the Eucharist and to make the presence of Christ perceptible in the congregation through the hospitality, compassion, and contemplative prayer of its members. Monasteries first came into existence when parishes no longer provided an adequate environment to achieve these objectives.

The spirituality of the local parish needs to be renewed in our time. Monasteries are few while the hunger for a deeper life of prayer and a structure to support it goes on increasing. The local parish needs to become once again a scriptural environment, a community where the word of God is being presented and transmitted by the teaching and witness of qualified teachers.

Contemplation is the capacity to listen to the word of God at the deepest level. It is from this space that the Eucharist should be celebrated and the various ministries of the local community carried out. Christian spirituality responds to the marked hunger for a deeper knowledge and experience of God that is spreading among lay persons across denominational boundaries. Yet little is heard on the parish level about the Christian religion as a life to be lived, a relationship with God to be developed and enjoyed. The most important fruit of seminary training should be a thorough knowledge, understanding, and experience of the spiritual journey in the Christian tradition so that the leaders of Christian churches can be recognized as men and women of deep prayer, and at the same time can transmit the Christian life as experience.

The hunger for spiritual experience is also surfacing in other world religions. It will be even more common in the future. It is essential that priests and ministers be prepared by training and practice to meet this development as well as to cope with its counterfeits. The ignorance of the spiritual journey has been monumental in recent centuries. In this book, Father William Meninger, who first developed a practical method of communicating the teaching of *The Cloud of Unknowing* to people of our time, describes the stages of contemplative prayer and its fruits. He provides examples of the kind of information and inspiration that should be available on a regular basis in every Christian community.

Thomas Keating, OCSO

There are evidently four kinds of monks. The first are the cenobites, that is, those who live in monasteries, serving under a rule and an abbot.

from the Rule of St. Benedict, chap. 1

CHAPTER ONE

ARCHETYPE MONKS

THERE IS AN ORGANIZATION IN Aspen, Colorado called the Aspen Institute for Humanistic Studies. Founded by the philosopher Mortimer Adler, it periodically calls together executives from businesses all over the world to meet and discuss the humanities, philosophy, religion and ethics—in other words, subjects that they as businessmen and -women are not usually exposed to. Often, as a part of the "Aspen experience," these groups make a visit to our monastery to attend our evening

Vespers and Eucharistic liturgy, and to chat with the monks about our "alternative lifestyle." Most of them are not Catholic and have never before visited a monastery.

A letter received recently from an IBM executive after one such visit stated: "I am not a Catholic, possibly not even a Christian, I have never visited a monastery before and do not completely understand what I saw there or how it has affected me, but I know I am permanently changed—and for the better." Why is this? Why should a single brief visit to a monastery have such a powerful effect? Why are people so fascinated by monks and by things monastic?

One evening, Fr. Theophane and I met with a group from the Aspen Institute. They seemed to be interested in every aspect of monastic living, and the questions were coming fast and furious long after the time allotted had expired. Taking advantage of a brief pause in the barrage of questions, Fr. Theophane remarked: "See how interested you all are in the monastic life. There is a reason for this. Something of the monk exists in every one of us." I think this is a statement of profound truth. According to Carl Jung, there exist in all of us myths or archetypes which are the forms whereby our collective unconscious represents for itself the fundamental meanings of our basic relationships. Thus there exists in each one of us something of the Man, the Woman, the King, the Evil One, the Monk, etc. It is this element of the Monk in each of us that resonates to the silence, austerity, prayer, poverty, simplicity and obedience somehow tasted in even a brief visit to a monastery.

The days are gone, I think, when the whole Church saw the monastic life as her ideal model. There are many other models, spiritualities, or theological systems that relate more and more authentically to life in this modern world. Yet monastic spirituality will always have its place. It will always speak to something that lies deep in the innermost being of every man and woman of every culture and religious belief. The Franciscan liberation theologian Leonardo Boff says that Jesus will not allow himself to be domesticated by any particular theological system. What Jesus tells us of God is too great to be comprehended and explained by any one form of spirituality. Jesus is the Word that must be spoken over and over again in every age, to every people, and in every culture. He is colored by every situation (so Jesus is black in Africa, yellow in Asia, white in Europe), fully expressed by none, touched upon by all.

Yet there is something of this Word which is Jesus that is spoken in the center of our beings and that reaches a recognizable expression in the monastic life. This is why monasticism is a viable witness and why it finds a resonating chord in so many men and women.

For some the words "monastic" and "contemplative" are almost synonymous. To be a monk is to be a contemplative, to witness to the value of contemplation and to share this value with those who resonate to it and wish to support and strengthen it in themselves. This sharing is indeed a viable part of monastic spirituality, and is the reason why we Trappist monks write books and even occasionally leave our monasteries to give conferences, workshops, and retreats. But above all, our witness is in the living, in the abiding communal expression of the contemplative attitude.

Here at St. Benedict's we specify and intensify our monastic witness to contemplation by an hour-long period of meditation each morning after the night office of Vigils. The meditation is held in the darkened church. Once it has begun, at 4 A.M., no one enters or leaves. At 4:30 there is a brief change of pace expressed in a slow, Zen-like walking meditation for about ten minutes, followed by a final twenty minutes of silent meditation. For some, there is another period of communal meditation at six in the evening, and lengthier periods during our frequent days of recollection and personal retreats.

The world has become a global village. The mass media brings the woes of billions of people in hundreds of countries to our daily attention. This is so even in our monastery where the media are severely restricted. Nonetheless we are constantly presented with the concrete personal sufferings of countless people.

On the bulletin board in our periodical room we post the numerous letters we receive begging for prayers, many of them poignant enough to break your heart. On a table in the same room are the requests we get from different charities, missionary orders, and lay groups dedicated to performing the corporal and spiritual works of mercy in the thousands of needy places throughout the world. All need prayers. All need funds to accomplish their work. How can one person or any one community of persons respond to these thousands of cries for help?

We help concretely wherever we can. We have an alms committee which disburses, throughout the year, a percentage of our income to selected charities. But as the apostles said to Jesus: "What are five loaves and two fishes among so many?"

Perhaps monastic spirituality offers something of an answer to those who are perplexed by the same great problem. We begin by distributing the loaves and the fishes, the funds, however small they may be. But with them goes more than material resources. With them go our finite hearts ever striving to be filled with infinite love. With them goes the dedication of our very lives, seeking daily to advance the Kingdom, not merely on a one-to-one basis, but with the realization that as we singly progress toward union with God we bring with us the whole Body of Christ, indeed the whole world.

A few weeks ago a young lady, a peace activist (or, better, a peace witness), came to our monastery for a retreat prior to performing a prophetic act of peace witnessing at the atomic weapons plant of Rocky Flats in Denver. She sent us the following letter:

Dear Monks,

Last month at a peace conference I was asked to give a five-minute speech on why I do civil disobedience. I was sick of words so I gave a one-minute speech instead. I wanted to share it with you because I will be seeking to amplify and refine these ideas during my time of solitude. Out of that I will act at Rocky Flats.

The big question that I'm struggling with is: how do I live in and out of the existential reality of the Resurrection of Christ in these times of crisis?

I really don't take my cues on how to live from the bomb. I don't act out of fear, despair, or desperation. My hope is solely founded on the belief that the Resurrection is efficacious in our time. Christ has the final word over the bomb. In fact, the bomb does not exist outside the world which Christ created and continues to uphold moment by moment by his Power and Love.

The bomb is a manifestation of the evil which has been overcome. Christ's Realm has begun and we are invited and challenged by Christ to participate with him in his redemptive act which continues through history.

So when I go to a nuclear weapons plant to pray for peace, my prayer is a prayer of celebration and a proclamation of the efficacy of Christ's Resurrection over the illusory power of the bomb.

It is my hunch, and I am experimenting with this, that to dance and celebrate in the midst of Babylon has the potential (if Christ so blesses it) of turning Babylon into the New Jerusalem. But for the celebration to be genuine and authentic, it must come out of a heart open and vulnerable to the world's suffering.

May God grant us such a heart and teach us to dance celebratively and victoriously.

I don't think you could find anywhere a more profound understanding and expression of what Christ's victory means and what our share in that victory involves!

When I was a young seminarian in my first year of studies for the diocesan priesthood, I learned that another seminarian in the class ahead of me had left to join the Trappists. While still a novice, he was afflicted with an incurable form of cancer, and we students kept a kind of prolonged death-watch. We were kept informed by frequent visits of the seminary rector to Brother Clement's monastic infirmary bed at St. Joseph's Abbey in Spencer, Massachusetts. I remember how pleased the students in his class were when the rector announced that Bro. Clement had dedicated his monastic life (and death—which was to follow shortly) to the advancement and success of their priestly ministry! Fifteen years later, when I was about to join the same Trappist community, a fellow priest from my seminary class reminded me of Bro. Clement's promise and asked me if I would do the same for the class of priests ordained with me.

Even I was surprised at the swiftness of my refusal. I did not want to limit myself so severely! I wanted to embrace the whole world. I wanted to be a part of the ministry of every priest or nun in every parish or mission in the world. I wanted to feed all the hungry, visit all the sick and imprisoned, shelter all the homeless, instruct all the ignorant, counsel all the doubtful and console all the sorrowing of all the world.

In my monastic commitment I was to find the means of doing this. I would dedicate my personal search for God to the ministry of the whole Body of Christ. Their work would be my work, their failures would be my burdens, their successes would be my triumphs. I would minister to the sick through every doctor, nurse, orderly, or worried parent. I would teach through every teacher, feed the hungry through every farmer, store clerk, waitress or cook. In my search for God I would be limited only by the limitations of his divine love and compassion. I am not intimidated because I have only five loaves and a few fish. I know what Jesus can do with them.

After I finished my two-year novitiate and some five years in temporary vows at St. Joseph's Abbey, I went out to our hermitage in the woods for an eight-day retreat in order to prepare for final, solemn vows. On my first day, I sat down with pen and paper and wrote all the reasons I could think of for committing myself to solemn vows. I filled many, many sheets of paper. On the second day, I started eliminating reasons I felt were superficial or trivial. Each day for seven days I rewrote my reasons until by the eighth day, at the end of my retreat, I had the briefest, most essential expression of what my solemn vows were to mean. Here is what I see as the witness of monastic life, in the formula I composed for my solemn vows:

It would be almost impossible to enumerate the many values and motives that proclaim the meaning of the commitment to the monastic life. This is because these values are based upon the infinite potentialities of God's grace in a given individual. However, the occasion of solemn profession demands that I make some attempt.

I seek the monastic commitment because it is a further specification of my baptismal vows. It is the beginning of the eschatological experience of that everlasting life which faith brings and which baptism promises. I seek it, not only as the reaffirmation of Christian maturity, which all must bring to their baptismal commitment, but also as a further determination of personal, charismatic response to God's grace as it manifests itself in His call to a life of prayer, solitude, silence, and joyful penance.

I seek the monastic life in an order and in a monastery totally dedicated to prayer, because this call of God in his awesome transcendency is an experience in the light of which one can only stand before him in wonder—a wonder which must ultimately manifest itself in contemplative prayer . . . also because the call of God in his immanent presence in the Church must be responded to by a dedicated service of love and obedience in community.

I seek this particular type of monastic commitment as a witness to the risen Lord so intense, immediate, and imperative that it has no time for anything else—even for other good things.

And finally, I seek the monastic life under the authority of an abbot as a spiritual father and in this community as a school of the Lord's service, as a dedicated gathering of Christian brethren with whom to identify, love, and honor in a common way of life and with whom I seek God's honor and glory in all things. And so . . .

Before God and his saints whose relics are venerated here at St. Joseph's Abbey, and in the presence of the Abbot, I, William Austin Meninger, of the priestly order, promise stability, conversion of manners, and obedience according to the Rule of our holy father Benedict.

CHAPTER TWO

St. Anthony

St. Anthony the Great was 105 years old when he died c. 355 A.D. Shortly after his death, Athanasius, the bishop of Alexandria, wrote his biography. It was actually intended to be a rule for monks, but instead of listing a number of regulations, Athanasius presented Anthony as the perfect example for monastic living. The biography quickly became popular, and was responsible for thousands of monastic vocations in the ensuing decades and centuries.

Anthony lived before the establishment of monasteries. In his day, an individual wanting to live the ascetical life simply went to the outskirts of a town and lived as a kind of semi-hermit. Anthony joined such a group and worked assiduously, imitating the virtues which he saw as outstanding in particular hermits. Thus he vied with one in fasting, with another in prayer, and with still another in holy silence, until he excelled them all and could learn nothing more from them. Then he moved on.

Anthony went out into the desert some distance from the town. Here he dwelt for twenty years in a tomb where he underwent most of his famous temptations. Since the fourth century, these temptations have been a most popular subject for paintings by great artists, who have delighted in letting their imaginations run riot in depicting the multitude of horrendous imps, demons, and devils afflicting St. Anthony in myriad ways and manners.

Having successfully battled these evil beings for twenty years, Anthony emerged from the tomb. After the long years of fasting, praying, and fighting demons, Athanasius reports that Anthony was in perfect health—even retaining a full set of teeth! His search for spiritual perfection had resulted in a perfect man both in body and soul. Somehow Anthony managed to overcome the evil effects of Adam's sin, and his spirituality was holistic. Not only did he reestablish in his life dominion over the evil one, he also overcame the curse of illness and physical deterioration. Even later in his life, when Anthony retired further into the inner mountain, he was to overcome the loss of mastery due to Adam's sin to such an extent that he even eventually recovered Adam's dominion over the animals.

Anthony is said to have gone into the desert for the same reasons that Jesus went into the wilderness. This was not to flee from the world, but to wrestle with the devil.

What happened to Jesus during his forty days in the wilder-

ness of Judea? He was tempted by the devil. The three temptations described in Matthew's Gospel represent the full gamut of
evils that man is subject to. Jesus overcame them all in a decisive
manner, but it yet remained for him to live out his life in accord
with his rejection of Satan and his affirmations of his Sonship
with God. We are told explicitly by St. Luke that when Jesus' forty
days were over, the devil departed from him—for a while! He
would be definitively conquered only by Jesus' Resurrection.

St. Anthony realized, as we all must, that Jesus has won the
victory for us, but we must, individually, reach out and claim it.

In selecting Anthony as a model for monks, St. Athanasius
realized that monks were basically good people and that good
people are not attracted to evil—or, at least, are able to recognize
and fight such attractions. What monks could be attracted by,
Athanasius realized, was a temptation to good, a temptation to
be lured into the performance of some lesser good than they
were called to by their monastic vocation. To fight this kind of
temptation, it is necessary to recognize it for what it is. This
requires both maturity and counsel.

See how this awareness was acted out in Anthony's life. One
day he was walking along a road leading through the desert. All
of a sudden as he turned a bend, he saw that the road ahead of
him was literally covered with hundreds of solid gold nuggets.
Anthony's eyes lit up and his heartbeat increased as he realized
the power that would be his (and, of course, the good that he
could do) with such enormous wealth. But then he stopped and
thought: what was all that gold doing scattered on a public road
out in the desert? It was not possible that someone could have
lost so much wealth and not been aware of it. Therefore it must
have been put there deliberately as a temptation—or, worse still,
it was only an illusion of the devil and was not there at all.
Without even touching the gold, Anthony fled.

The next day, as Anthony continued along the road, he had another temptation. He saw the ground in front of him covered with silver nuggets. This time he knew that they were real. It was no illusion, and no reasoning process could convince him that it was. Without even touching the silver, Anthony fled.

What was the difference between these two temptations, and what does Athanasius wish to teach us by reporting them? Notice that in both cases the evil, if there was any evil, was not obvious. Gold and silver are not evil and, indeed, can be used to do much good. The gold was illusion but the silver was real. It is important to notice that Anthony recognized this difference. It is also important to notice that his reaction to both was the same: he fled.

The gold which was illusion represents temptations which are illusory. Indeed, are not most temptations such? Our imaginations, or our baser appetites, will present overwhelming pictures, sounds, smells or whatever, to such an extent that our judgment is affected and we can be led into the most unloving and self-destructive activity possible. Anthony was mature enough to recognize illusion and to flee from it. It was an illusory temptation against his commitment to the monastic life, under the guise of something good.

Such temptations are common enough both in and out of monasteries. How often young monks (especially when in the throes of the inevitable cleansing temptations of the monastic life—the wrestling with the devil) will turn their eyes toward greener pastures. Visions of the good they could do as a parish priest, as a parent, as a missionary, as a social worker, dance before them. If these are illusory, how can they be dealt with? Are they temptations or are they calls from God? Are the nuggets real or not? See how they are tempted not to evil but to good—for them, a lesser good, if God is calling them to the monastic life.

Here they need the aid of their own maturity or, lacking that, of mature advice. It is precisely to conquer such illusory temptations that we require a certain maturity and experience on the part of our candidates. If they have not already had such experience, we urge them to get involved in some apostolic endeavors or some service work such as that done by hospital orderlies, soup kitchen volunteers, or Confraternity of Christian Doctrine (CCD) instructors. Then, when such temptations arise in the context of their monastic life, they will recognize whether or not they are illusions and flee them.

The silver nuggets which were real represent temptations which are real. Each of us has to determine how such temptations affect his or her own life. For monks, such temptations can take the form of strong attractions to married life, the love of children, or the desire to be of more active service to God's people. They can also involve an attraction to any of the good things not normally involved in the monastic regimen. When a genuine vocation is at stake, the monk must again follow Anthony's advice and flee.

Anthony and the early monks literally went out into the desert to wrestle with the devil. This always included confronting themselves and penetrating the artificial facade of the false self—a lengthy, exhausting, but worthwhile struggle. This is a positive move. It is not so much a running from the world (because, in the last analysis, we bring the world with us), but a fleeing toward something, toward a direct confrontation with the forces in ourselves and about us that are not-God.

Such a struggle is difficult to engage in successfully on an individual basis. Notice that Anthony did not go into solitude in the tomb until he had gotten all that was possible of support, instruction, and imitation from the holy men around his village. In the Benedictine tradition, monks are warned not to

aspire to the eremitical life until they have gotten all of the wisdom, maturity, and strength that can possibly be obtained from
their communities.

CHAPTER THREE

RELATIONSHIPS

IT HAS BEEN ALMOST TEN years now since I came to St. Benedict's from our motherhouse of St. Joseph's Abbey. Initially I came here for two months, to help out for the summer. There were then only eight monks in the community. My first assignment was as vocation director. In two months I could only begin to direct the potential candidates who were making their first visits to the monastery during the summer months, so I had to extend my stay in Snowmass to six months, then to a year.

Finally, three years later, bowing to the inevitable signs of God's will, I changed my stability with the blessings of both the abbots from Spencer and Snowmass.

Trappist monks, like Benedictines, follow the Rule of St. Benedict. Our interpretation of the Rule stems from a reform movement begun by St. Robert of Molesmes, around 1100 A.D. at Citeaux in France. From the name of St. Robert's monastery, we are called Cistercians. Centuries later there was another reform at the monastery of La Trappe. From the name of that monastery, we are also known as Trappists.

According to the Rule, monks must take three vows: obedience, conversion of manners, and stability (canonically, there are five vows; poverty and chastity are included implicitly in the vow of conversion of manners). Conversion of manners concerns itself with a lifestyle according to the Rule, and also involves a certain attitude by which a monk commits himself to a monastic lifestyle. Stability involves a commitment for life to one particular monastery. There can be reasons for changing one's place of stability, however, such as supplying necessary help for daughterhouses, as I did.

The vow of stability in our order is very important and influences the procedures we follow in screening candidates. We do not consider vocational candidates as being called to the order as such, but rather as being called to a particular house of the order. For this reason, when candidates come to Snowmass for an initial visit, we usually insist that they then visit one or two other Trappist houses before returning here.

Because of my personal experiences in both a small house (even now, Snowmass has only 17 monks), and a large one (Spencer and Gethsemani are usually nearly equal in being the largest houses in the order with something over 90 monks), I usually direct candidates toward visiting a larger monastery. The sociological differences between a large and small community are very significant, and most people seem quite clearly attracted to one or the other.

There are definite advantages to a large house, and when I first became a monk, I did not feel the slightest attraction to a small monastery. Large communities have greater reserves of talent, thus they are able to have a full course of theological studies available to their monks. Also, because of talent and sheer numbers, they are able to perform more elaborate and richer liturgical functions. This may or may not appeal to an individual. Often the work scene benefits because of the number of monks. The work is more diversified, thus providing more varied outlets and more opportunities for fresh changes of occupation.

On the other hand, small monastic communities have their own advantages. The liturgy tends to be simpler. The work situation is usually more demanding and requires a greater maturity and a wider range of responses from each monk. Most important, though, is the matter of personal relationships.

Relationships among the members of any community are crucial. This is the locus where monks are expected to carry out the great commandment of love which is the primary expression of the Christian vocation. The dynamics of relationships are matters of great concern in our present culture. As a result, smaller, intimate groupings or communities are in great favor. It is, of course, possible to have the most ideal relationships in both a large community and a small one. However, the larger the community, the more difficult it becomes to have any kind of intimate relationship with all the members. In a small community, when personal difficulties arise, they must be faced and brought to a loving solution if any kind of adequate Christian living situation is to be maintained. If the community is large enough, however, personal difficulties in relationships can often be avoided simply by hiding in numbers.

Loving relationships, of course, are a matter of concern for all of us in every family, monastic or not. Loving relationships are what make human beings; they are methods by which we recognize the Christ-nature in one another and by which we teach and draw out from one another the unspeakably great gifts of God's potential in each one of us.

I can never forget an experience I had as a young seminarian on my first visit to a mental hospital. The psychiatrist who was showing me around took me into a room that, on first viewing, seemed empty. It took a moment or two to notice the thirty-year-old man hiding in the corner. He was sitting on the floor with his head bowed on his knees and his arms wrapped around his legs in the fetal position. He was presented by the psychiatrist as an extreme case of catatonia, a total withdrawal from the world back to the womb.

When we left the room, we discussed at least some of the possibilities that had led this man to such a degree of withdrawal. The scenario could have been something like this: A child came into the world as supposedly the fruit of a loving relationship. He had, at the time, nothing but needs—a need to be fed, clothed, cleaned, cuddled and loved. Presumably he was given the usual personnel of the human community: a mother, father, and perhaps others, to supply those needs. As the individual needs came upon him, he would reach out, consciously or unconsciously, to those who, out of their loving relationship, had the responsibility to respond to them.

One day, he reached out with a need, and instead of a loving response, he was ignored or rebuked or punished. Reacting even unconsciously to this unloving response, the next time he had a need, he reached out less confidently, with hesitation and even some fear. He "asked his father for bread and was handed a stone!" Now he would reach out only when his need was extreme and sometimes not even then.

As he grew, he withdrew. The loving relationships so necessary to draw out his own loving potential were not there. Further and further he would withdraw from the world, becoming more and more catatonic—withdrawing completely from his hateful world to the only real and secure comfort he had ever known, the womb.

We have an awesome responsibility to love one another. Our very humanity depends upon it. What a frightful thing it is to realize that we go about our daily lives loving or unloving, giving life or death. Is not unloving, after all, the only sin? It all comes down to an unloving relationship with oneself, with God, or with our neighbor.

Have we not had, each one of us, the experience of responding in an unloving way? of giving death when we have been asked for life? of being the cause of someone who had a right to expect love receiving indifference or even hatred, and subsequently withdrawing from us, reaching out less confidently, becoming dehumanized? What can we do about this? How can we realize the full potential of those about us, bring them to the full stature of their development in Christ?

We must first remember that charity begins at home. The emphasis is on the word "begins." If we do not experience, share, respond to, and initiate loving relationships with those closest to us in our homes and communities, where will they begin?

In his play *Our Town*, Thornton Wilder illustrates this point beautifully. The plot is very simple. It involves the ordinary daily lives of George Gibbs and Emily Webb, who grow up as childhood sweethearts and marry shortly after high-school graduation. A year or two later, Emily dies in childbirth. An important scene takes place at her funeral, which we view from the vantage point of those who died before her and who are in the cemetery taking part in a purgatorial cleansing while waiting for their attachments to earthly life to diminish.

Emily, who has just died, is very attached to her earthly life, and greatly distressed as she observes the sorrow of her husband and her family. Suddenly she becomes aware that she has the power to return. She can go back as a kind of spirit and watch the reliving of her earthly life, or any part of it she wishes. Against the advice of her dead companions, who are obviously experienced in these ways, she decides to return, but as a concession to their pleadings, determines to return for only one day. They convince her to select an utterly insignificant day—one so unimportant that she cannot even remember it. She chooses a day that has completely escaped her memory, a day many years previous—her thirteenth birthday.

Together with a companion (the stage manager of the play), Emily goes back over the years to her mother's house, and steps into the scene as both Emily the thirteen year-old and Emily the ghost. Her very first reaction is traumatic. She marvels at how young her mother looks, and wonders why we ever have to grow old.

Emily is greatly excited by her return after the tragedy and sorrow of her death, and approaches her mother with great emotion, putting out her arms to embrace her. Her mother, however, is actually living the single reality of the thirteenth birthday and does not notice. She pecks her on the cheek without showing any real emotion, and wishes her a happy birthday while turning to the stove to putter over breakfast. Emily, unheard by her mother, pleads with her, "Mother, please look at me for one minute as though you really saw me."

Emily is now in tears and barely able to carry on. All of the things, odors, sights, sounds, and especially people that she had taken for granted assume new importance. Relationships, especially, now lost, are most precious. In an agonized appeal, she turns to the unmoved stage manager: "It all goes so fast, we don't have time to look at one another." Remember, this was just an ordinary day in Emily's life, one she could not even recall! Upon hearing her father's voice in the background, Emily finally breaks down and pleads to be taken back to the cemetery to her grave. First, however, she turns to her mother and to the dear familiar objects of her childhood throughout the room. She says goodbye to all of them and flings her arms wide in an ecstasy of realization as she exclaims, "O world, you're too wonderful for anyone to realize you!" Then she turns to the stage manager and asks reflectively, "Does anyone ever realize the world while he lives it, every, every minute?" "No," the stage manager replies, and then adds, "Saints and poets, maybe. They do, some."

We are called to be saints, we are called to realize the world. We are called to see and appreciate the magnificence of all loving relationships. We are called to look at our family, at our community, at our world every, every minute as though we really saw them.

CHAPTER FOUR

NAME THEOLOGY

IT IS EARLY IN THE morning. The whole community is gathered, seated in a circle in the chapter room. In the middle of the circle, extending out from the abbot's feet, is a rectangular multicolored rug woven some years ago by Bro. Bernard. Its colors are those of the earth and sky as reflected during the different seasons of the year in our beautiful Colorado valley.

This rug has had a central place in every significant ceremony at our monastery for many years. On it has lain the bier containing the bodies of our brothers. Prostrate upon it, Bro. Raymond heard the chanting of the community as he pronounced his solemn vows. Our abbot, too, humbled himself before the Lord on this rug, as he received from our bishop the abbatial blessing. Every monk in the past eight years to make simple vows, every new member received into the community, and every postulant to receive the monastic habit in our clothing ceremony prostrated on this rug as he sought entrance into the community and the order.

This morning we are having one such clothing ceremony. When the community is assembled and the abbot gives the signal, the novice master arises and goes to the chapel where Bro. James is waiting in prayer. He leads Bro. James into the midst of the circle and waits beside him while James prostrates on the rug and answers the abbot's questions: "What do you seek?" "The mercy of God," Brother answers, "and of the order." "Rise, in the name of the Lord," the abbot responds, and Bro. James rises and goes to his seat. The abbot now gives a brief homily, welcomes Bro. James into the community, and announces to the monks the name by which Bro. James has chosen to be known in his monastic career.

The taking of a new name, different from the one given in baptism, was once a common practice. Its purpose was to indicate that the new monk was beginning a new life and becoming a new person. However, today a different element is stressed. Monastic life is considered to be a continuation of the baptismal life, a further specification of one's Christian life, and not necessarily a radical change from Christian living. The present tendency, therefore, is to keep one's baptismal name, although for those who find it helpful, a new name is usually permitted. There is also a tendency today towards double names, especially if someone in the community already has one's baptismal name.

(Thus we have a number of monks with double names, such as Matthew-James or Edward-Joseph.)

To answer the question: "What's in a name?" we have to turn to what is sometimes called name theology. It involves a look at the fascinating biblical custom of giving, receiving, and changing names.

We see the workings of name theology even in the book of Genesis. The very names of Adam and Eve are indicative of their origins and mission: "from-the-earth," and "mother-of-all-who-live." When Adam was allowed to name the animals, this was to indicate that he had authority and power over them. He pointed out, and maybe even helped to determine, their natures.

To know someone's name meant to have power over him. There are still primitive tribes in the world who have elaborate systems of taboos governing secret names precisely to avoid a dangerous domination of one person over another. In these tribes, as in the biblical milieu, to speak someone's name was to touch upon his very being. Even today we make a distinction between someone's formal name (usually beginning with their title: Mr. or Mrs., Father, Brother, Sister), and their personal names. To use personal names often implies closeness or affection, and implies a corresponding powerful influence over the person.

In the Scriptures, God often named his chosen prophets in order to indicate their mission and sometimes their authority. Children were often named to indicate their relation to God. Thus Hannah named her son Samuel: "Because," she said, "I asked the Lord for him" (the name being derived from the Hebrew verb sha'al—to ask). Hosea's children were named by the Lord Lo-ruhamah (Not-loved) and Lo-ammi (Not my people), as prophetic gestures, to indicate his displeasure with his people. At an important point in their history, Abraham and

Sarah received new names, as did Jacob, to indicate something of their divine missions.

The greatest name of all was spoken to Moses when he was sent from the mountain of God to rescue his people from Pharaoh:

> Then Moses said to God, "If I go to the Israelites and tell them that the God of their forefathers has sent me to them, and they ask me his name, what shall I say?" God answered, "I am; that is who I am. Tell them that I AM (Yahweh) has sent you to them. This is my name forever; this is my title in every generation" (Ex. 3:13).

In a sense, Moses now had power even over God. He knew his name and was commissioned to use it. This knowledge marked him as an ambassador and allowed him to speak in God's name. So sacred was the name of Yahweh among the Jews that the utterance of it was punishable by death, and the reader of the Scriptures in Jewish worship services (even in modern times) is not allowed to read "Yahweh," but must substitute "Adonai" (the Lord).

It was the angel Gabriel who named the son of Elizabeth and Zechariah John. His mother was told this, and it was only when they observed the angel's command and named the child John that his father, who had been stricken dumb by Gabriel, was able to speak again.

At the Annunciation, Gabriel told Mary that her son's name would proclaim his mission. He was to be called Jesus, which means Savior. It only awaited St. Paul's letter to the Philippians (2:10) to give this name its proper deference:

> Therefore God raised him to the heights and bestowed on him the name above all names, that at the name of Jesus

every knee should bow—in heaven, on earth, and in the depths—and every tongue confess, "Jesus Christ is Lord," to the glory of God the Father.

Even the demons knew the power of a name, and often in the Gospels we see a scenario of power when Jesus confronts them. In the synagogue at Capernaum, while Jesus was teaching, there was a man possessed of an unclean spirit. Right away the spirit tried to assert control over Jesus by speaking his name. He shrieked, "What do you want with us, Jesus of Nazareth? Have you come to destroy us? I know who you are—the Holy One of God." Jesus silenced him first and then exorcised the man (Mk. 1:24).

In the country of the Gerasenes, the possessed man who lived among the tombs proclaimed the Lord's name: "What do you want with me, Jesus, Son of the Most High God? In God's name, do not torment me." Certainly the devils knew their name theology! But so did Jesus, as he asserted his power by demanding that the demons declare their name: "Jesus asked him, 'What is your name?' 'My name is Legion,' he said, 'There are so many of us' " (Mk. 10:6f.).

Jesus followed in the tradition of name theology when he changed Simon's name to Peter. This was to announce his mission to be the foundation-stone of the new people of God. So was Saul's Hebrew name dropped in favor of the Hellenic Paul when he changed his mission from the Jews to the Gentiles.

It was at the Sermon on the Mount that Jesus demonstrated most emphatically his understanding of name theology. You will recall that it was then that he revealed himself as the new Moses, the new lawgiver, combining the roles of Moses and Yahweh. He did not intend to change the Law but to fulfill it, to penetrate to its essential meaning, to go from the letter to the true spirit. He showed this by the language he used: "You have heard it said . . . but I say to you. . . ."

It was on a mountain that God revealed his name to Moses. He thereby established a relationship with Moses and, through Moses, with his people. He allowed Moses to have this power over him for the sake of his people, so that his people could be freed, liberated, brought from bondage to the promised land. So too, St. Matthew would have us understand, at the Sermon on the Mount, Jesus proclaimed our new relationship with God by using the very different name of Abba-Father. In chapters five, six, and seven of St. Matthew's Gospel, Jesus refers to God as Father no less than seventeen times. This, of course, includes his instruction on the Lord's Prayer, where he insists that "Our Father" is the name we should use in calling upon God.

This is the ultimate in name theology. Is there another name, term, or title that even God could give us to indicate greater intimacy, and a more loving sense of care? Is there a better way in which he could show us that he wants us to have power over him, that he would answer our prayers? The intimacy of the very Trinity itself is opened to us. The Son reveals to us the Father, and in the gracious power of the Holy Spirit shares him with us.

And what lies in store? Will God give us a different name? Will his love open up for us a future that the heart of man cannot even conceive?

> Hear, you who have ears to hear, what the Spirit says to the churches! To him who is victorious I will give some of the hidden manna; I will give him also a white stone, and on the stone will be written a new name, known to none but him who receives it.

> (Rev. 2:17)

CHAPTER FIVE

BROTHER BERNARD

———◆———

"BROTHER BERNIE IS DEAD!" How stark were the words. How irreversible! Far too serious to be a joke, once uttered, we had no choice but to hear them as truth, and our world was forever changed. That is how we felt on that freezing February morning when we heard how Bro. Bernie had suddenly dropped dead on the sidewalk from a massive heart attack shortly after finishing with his dental appointment in Aspen.

Oh yes, it was an easy way to go. No suffering, no lingering illness, no dying—only death. But we monks who were his community, who loved him, who were left behind, what did it do to us? But is not this what the monastic life is all about? After all, we Trappists are the ones who have inherited the tradition, as described by the popular press, of heavily cowled monks passing one another in darkened cloisters with a mutually muttered, "Remember death, Brother."

Above all, however, we have inherited the tradition of being human. As humans we felt the loss of Bernie's presence and were reminded of our own precarious hold on life. How was it possible that such infectious joy could suddenly be snuffed out? For thirty-five years Bro. Bernard had presided over the monastery kitchen with patience, loving service, and culinary imagination. Indeed, in the years that I had been a part of St. Benedict's monastery, I had not yet experienced the full range of his imaginative recipes, nor failed to be uplifted by his constant examples of loving service.

Many of us recalled the rather extraordinary statement that the abbot had made only a few months earlier. "I think," he said, "that Bro. Bernie could die at any moment. I don't know if he could grow any further in love. He is just biding time." When this prophecy was uttered, Bernie, in his early fifties, was in perfect health.

Bro. Bernard did not fit into any mold. Most of his monastic life (he entered at the age of 18) was spent under the extremely rigid, penitential Trappist observances. A monk was not expected to be different; a good monk was one who fit into a mold. Bernie was a good monk who did not. His strong personality and original outlook would never allow him to be submerged by the mountains of observances, rules and regulations of his monastic calling.

His cheerful grin—he had one tooth missing up front—and the ever-present Irish twinkle in his eyes were infectious, and had a way of intruding themselves into the most somber monastic occasions. His sense of humor was boundless. He used it frequently to penetrate the barriers of hypocrisy, self-love, unkind exaggerations or criticisms that he might sense, even as indirect innuendoes, in the conversations or attitudes of his brothers. Whenever he heard a criticism leveled against anyone, his invariable response would be, "Wouldn't it be funny if he were closer to God than we were!"

He abounded in malapropisms. Some of our favorites were:

"He was running around like a chicken with its legs cut off."
"Watch out, that water is red hot!"
"A bird in the bush is worth two in the hand."
"Don't throw stones at glass houses."
"She smoked like a fish."

In addition to being community cook, Bro. Bernie was our organist, our tailor, and the general factotum for all the odds and ends hanging loose in the monastic environment which no one else wanted or thought to do. He had a way of appreciating beautiful things which was easily and frequently communicated. Many of us were used to viewing our beautiful Rocky Mountain environment through his eyes and having our own appreciation enhanced through his mediation. Always near at hand was a pair of binoculars (referred to by Bernie as "spy glasses") which he would frequently hand around to point out the elk in the far oat field or the deer on the hillside beneath our water tower. Visitors coming to the monastery for the second time invariably asked for him, remembering his kindness and gracious hospitality. He could always spare a few moments to show them around.

And now he was dead. His body, clothed in the ample white monastic cowl, the habit of our order, was received by the community in the entrance room and placed on the simple wooden bier. We could hear the noise of the back-hoe coming from the hill to the front and right side of the monastery as Bro. David prepared his grave site. We carried him in mournful procession down the cloisters to the church where we placed his body before the altar, lit the Paschal candle, and knelt in silent prayer for our departed brother.

Monastic funerals, in my experience, are generally not sad affairs, but this was an exception. For the next two days, the priests who celebrated the community Masses during the vigil period before the burial paused often to clear choking voices or to wipe the tears from their eyes. Finally, when the time came, we took from the church wall the simple wooden cross that had been hanging there since the last funeral. It would be carried to lead the procession to our cemetery and be placed on the grave site as a marker awaiting the Resurrection. A new cross would be placed on the chapel wall until another monk died.

Cistercian burial rites are simple, but impressive. Monks are buried without a coffin. The hood of the cowl is folded over the face, and the body is lowered into the grave to be received into the arms of the infirmarian, who arranges it in a final loving service. The abbot places the first shovelful of earth on the body. Then his brothers fill the grave by shoveling the earth onto the body's feet, letting it gradually and indirectly cover the whole body. Then all withdraw.

Bro. Bernie was one of the Ancients. This is a very difficult word to explain. While it doesn't specifically have anything to do with age, one usually does not become an Ancient without spending many years in faithful monastic living. No one knows just how long it takes, nor can anyone put his finger on just when the change from ordinary monk to Ancient occurs. Everybody knows which monks are Ancients, but nobody can say just when they become so or how. One monk can be an Ancient at fifty, another at seventy, still another not until eighty.

An Ancient is not what a monk does but rather what a monk is; it is something that radiates from his very being and that manifests itself in everything he does. It shows in the way he says, "Thank you!" It reveals itself in his smile, in the depth of his stillness at prayer, his patience in illness and his fidelity to the small daily duties of his community service.

Not everyone becomes an Ancient. It is the end product of a life given over to faith, hope, love, and prayerful service. When it is there, you know it. Bro. Alfred was an Ancient, but not always. The change was discernable over twenty years as his love grew, his patience blossomed, and his goodness overflowed into the smallest details of his daily relationships. To see him shuffling through the cloisters with his ever-present rosary in hand and to receive his beatific smile and friendly greeting was a blessing. Fr. Vincent was an Ancient. It was a privilege to bring him his breakfast tray just to hear the sincerity of his gratitude and to see his enduring prayerful patience as he suffered, not without joy, through his long and fatal illness.

Fr. Anselm was an Ancient with a vengeance. The victim of frequent ailments, he enjoyed each one of them as a promise that this life would pass away for a better one. His mind was always on God, and he loved nothing better than to ask each visitor for a holy word or a brief prayer to provide him with food for pious thought.

Obviously, the quality of being an Ancient is not limited to people in the monastic scene. Recently I saw a beautiful movie on Mother Teresa. Here is an Ancient par excellence, a blend of the profoundly wise and the innocently simple, a woman who would one day address a full assembly of the United Nations or receive the Nobel Peace Prize, and who, on the next, would cradle in her arms a dying leper on the streets of Calcutta.

In his treatise on contemplative prayer, the unknown author of *The Cloud of Unknowing* tells us to expect the qualities of an

Ancient to show themselves in persons given to prayer over a long period of years. He entitles his fifty-fourth chapter in this way: "That contemplation graces a man with wisdom and poise and makes him attractive in body and spirit." Then he goes on to make these marvelous observations:

> As a person matures in the work of love, he will discover that this love governs his demeanor befittingly both within and without. When grace draws a man to contemplation, it seems to transfigure him even physically, so that though he may be ill-favored by nature, he now appears changed and lovely to behold. His whole personality becomes so attractive that good people are honored and delighted to be in his company, strengthened by the sense of God he radiates.

We are all called to be Ancients. In fact, each of us should be at least partly on the way to this goal. It does not happen overnight; it is a gradual happening that comes from a continual response to grace showing itself in our loving service.

> And so, do your part to cooperate with grace and win this great gift, for truly it will teach the man who possesses it how to govern himself and all that is his. He will even be able to discern the character and temperament of others when necessary. He will know how to accommodate himself to everyone and (to the astonishment of all) even to inveterate sinners, without sinning himself. God's grace will work through him, drawing others to desire that very contemplative love which the Spirit awakens in him. His countenance and conversation will be rich in spiritual wisdom, fire and the fruits of love . . . (from *The Cloud of Unknowing*).

CHAPTER SIX

TRUE WISDOM

INDIA IS OUR MONASTERY CAT, though we are not quite sure if she belongs to us or if we belong to her. I say we are not sure because there is no doubt at all in her mind. We, the monastery, the ranch, and the entire valley exist only for her benefit. We definitely get the feeling that India uses us. In her cat-mind we exist for the sole purpose of filling her dish. We are also allowed to open the kitchen door a hundred times a day for her goings and comings. Possessing nothing, she lives as owner of all she surveys, and may well be the most integrated inhabitant of the monastery.

But then it seems that all the animals in this Eden Garden of the Rocky Mountains have the same attitude. Is this perhaps a reversal of roles stemming from original sin? Are the animals, once created to serve man, now his masters? It would certainly seem so to Bro. Benito when he arises before midnight in the sub-zero February night to see if the ewes need his help in dropping their lambs. The novices feel the same way, no doubt, when they, each in his turn, have to hurry down to the barnyard before our 3 A.M. night office to bring a bottle of warm milk to our first-born lamb, Agatha, who lost her mother at birth. Indeed, the normal course of our winter work-day here at St. Benedict's Monastery is spent mostly in the service of "our" animals: cows, horses, sheep, pigs, and chickens.

The wild animals are not any better. Obviously the herd of elk, two hundred strong, that appears almost miraculously in our oat field every October evening, feels that the property is theirs. Of course, they were here long before we were, but must they be so disdainful, hopping over our five-foot fences as though they did not exist? And the mule deer are not to be trusted either. By sheer numbers alone they lay claim to our land. After all, what can eighteen squatter monks say to eight hundred deer about living space?

And then there are the coyotes. Not only do they claim prior rights to our sheep, but loudly howl their ownership into the night air from the fields adjacent to our monastic cells. The snowshoe rabbits and the prairie dogs own our roads. The rabbits race our farm vehicles between the road and the irrigation ditches, while the prairie dogs dig their dens right in the middle of the roads. And the porcupines! Who ever told them that we were raising an acre of broccoli just for their supper? I'm sure Bro. Kevin hoped to convince them otherwise when he trapped eight of them in the garden last August. We won't even mention the owls who steal our piglets, nor the field mice who invade our greenhouse and try to homestead in this bonanza of succulent crops.

What does all this say to us? We have but to look at Psalm 104, which we sing in choir each week:

Thou dost make the springs break out in the gullies,
 so that their water runs between the hills.
The wild beasts all drink from them,
 the wild asses quench their thirst;
The birds of the air nest on their banks
 and sing among the leaves.
From the high pavilion thou dost water the hills;
 The earth is enriched by thy provision.
Thou makest grass to grow for the cattle,
 and green things for those who toil for man,
bringing bread out of the earth
 and wine to gladden men's hearts,
oil to make their faces shine
 and bread to sustain their strength…
When thou makest darkness and it is night,
 all the beasts of the forest come forth;
the young lions roar for their prey,
 seeking their food from God.
When thou makest the sun rise,
 they slink away and go to rest in their lairs;
but man comes out to his work,
 and to his labors until evening.
Countless are the things thou hast made, O Lord.

Perhaps, after all, we are not the masters that we think we are. Or maybe we have simply misunderstood what mastery is. Is it the mastery of domination, by which we stand above all creation and demand that it serve us at whatever cost? Or is it the kind of mastery which God has shown us in the Incarnation, whereby we become part of creation and contribute to a mutually beneficial service?

What a different kind of world this delineates for us; a holistic, ecological balance in which men and women take their rightful share—one of mastery because it is one of intelligent stewardship—in which they work together with all creation.

> Countless are the things thou hast made, O Lord.
>   Thou hast made all by thy wisdom;
> and the earth is full of thy creatures,
>   beasts great and small.

Adam was created from the earth. He is a part of it. Raised to mastery over all creatures because he is in the image and likeness of God, he uses that dominion and reflects that likeness by exercising the very wisdom of God, who tells him, "Be wise, my son, then you will bring joy to my heart" (Prov. 27:11).

How much we can learn from our fellow creatures. How perfectly they serve the Creator simply by being manifestations of his wisdom!

> Four things there are which are smallest on earth yet wise beyond the wisest: ants, a people with no strength, yet they prepare their store of food in the summer; rock-badgers, a feeble folk, yet they make their home among the rocks; locusts, which have no king, yet they all sally forth in detachments; the lizard, which can be grasped in the hand, yet is found in the palaces of kings (Prov. 30:24–28).

The ants, the rock-badgers, the locusts, and the lizard, all insignificant in the hierarchy of creation, serve God perfectly by their response to his wisdom. Men and women alone are free to sin, to be unloving, to abuse their mastery. We are a part of creation, but by reason of our intelligence we are its cutting edge. We are in the forefront and have much to say in determining its direction.

A few years ago we were privileged to receive a visit from Dr. Mortimer Adler, who summers in nearby Aspen. He spoke to us on the function and capacity of the human mind. There are, he told us, four levels of activity in the human mind. The first is information. The mind in this regard is like an encyclopedia or a computer; it gathers and stores information, a series of facts. The second level is knowledge. The mind takes the information or series of facts and categorizes them, puts them in order, gives them organization, value, and importance. (And now we are beyond the computer's capabilities.) The third level is understanding. The Scriptures tell us that "knowledge is the principal thing; therefore, get knowledge; but in all thy getting, get understanding." On this level we are enabled to live our knowledge, to have experience of it, to use it in our daily lives. Finally, the fourth and highest mental activity is wisdom. This enables us to see our information, knowledge, and understanding in the light of ultimate goals, in the view of eternity, from the very perspective of God. As God made all things in wisdom, so we must see creation and our part in it from the viewpoint of God's purpose. It is surely in this sense that we may understand Jesus' statement: "The kingdom of God is within you."

This is the kind of wisdom that goes beyond textbooks and universities. It was a basic part of the life of our Native Americans, who would not kill a deer for food without praying to its spirit to explain their need and their gratitude and who would permit nothing of their quarry to be wasted. This is the wisdom that comes from the simplicity of babes and infants. Unless we become like them, we shall not enter the kingdom of God. It is the fruit not so much of study as of prayer:

> My son, if you take my words to heart and lay up my commands in your mind, giving your attention to wisdom and your mind to understanding, if you summon discernment to your aid and invoke understanding, if you seek her out like silver and dig for her like buried treasure, then you will understand the fear of the Lord and attain to the knowledge of God; for the Lord bestows wisdom and teaches knowledge and understanding (Prov. 2:1–6).

"In wisdom the Lord founded the earth" (Prov. 3:13) and it is through the wise that he brings it to its appointed fullness. This fullness will manifest itself in the establishment of his kingdom, not only in the hearts of a few simple and wise people but eventually everywhere and in everyone.

As far as the heavens are from the earth, so far are God's ways from our ways. The kingdom will not be dependent on the great and powerful of this world but on the wise, the humble, and the simple. We see it now only in part and in a dark mirror, but we do see it, and we can enter into it, share it, and advance it. Each one of us has his or her place in bringing about the fullness of God's kingdom.

CHAPTER SEVEN

LECTIO DIVINA

THE SILENCE OF THE SCRIPTORIUM is a busy kind of thing. It is 5 A.M. Our large arched windows are still dark and it will be a further two hours before the light and warmth of the rising sun manage to look over the top of Monastery Peak and peer into our January lives. By then we shall be preparing for Mass. Meanwhile the monks, each in his own way, are generating their own light and warmth.

I know what the novices are reading; since I am the novice

master, they consult with me regularly. Bro. Carl is doing his Old Testament research. The entire Bible is new to him, and in the past six months since coming to the monastery, he has happily made the leap from summer-resort and vacation home real estate to the Garden of Eden, the Land of Goshen, and the forty-year trek through the Sinai Desert. It is refreshing to share his enthusiasm and to rediscover with him the story of God's involvement in human history.

With his head bent low and his eyes a few inches away from the book, Bro. Peter is avidly perusing the mystics. I was a monk for ten years before I opened John of the Cross. Peter brought his *Complete Works* with him when he entered a year ago. Any day now he will come to me to describe his experiences in the dark night of the soul, and I will have to remind him of St. John's warning to read his great work on the spiritual journey at least twice before making any personal applications. Yet I must not discourage him. The slow, patient process of spiritual growth is as gradual and yet as measurable as physical development. Unfortunately, however, it's not as simple as backing up against a wall and chalking down growth marks.

Richard is an observer—here only for a six-month discernment period—and is reading a history of the order, Louis Lekai's *The White Monks*. Next for him, I suppose, will be Thomas Merton's *The Waters of Siloe*, the history of most of our American houses. At this time, I don't know if I should encourage him rather into areas of personal development and let his specifically monastic interests wait for further discernment. He might be disappointed and apt to misinterpret my motives.

The book Bro. Robert is nodding over is, no doubt, the *American Catechism*. More than the others he needs some basic instruction in theology. He would rather be out feeding the sheep this cold winter morning, but is nonetheless willing to endure the plodding effort of being nourished himself in Christian doctrine.

Bro. Charles, by contrast, has an intellectual background, including a master's degree in philosophy. At my suggestion, he is reading William James' *Varieties of Religious Experience*. I read this myself only a few years ago, and heartily agree with Father Basset (*We Neurotics*) that it is one of the best books available on the subject. Written over eighty years ago, it is still fifty years ahead of the times. I am sure Bro. Charles will be influenced by it, as I was.

Others are reading books as diverse and interesting as are their own backgrounds and personalities. I am hard put, at times, to keep up with them. Our novitiate reading list is helpful but certainly not able to cover their vast expanse of interests and spiritual needs. We have many companions on the way who have successfully fought the fight and shared their strategies with us through their books.

The phrase we use for spiritual reading is "lectio divina." Literally, it means divine reading, but it involves a great deal more than mere reading. To emphasize this and to stress the prayer orientation of lectio divina, we accompany it by a ritual. It is one which I learned as a novice and continue to this day. We begin by kneeling down and offering a brief prayer. While still on our knees, we take up the book we are reading, read a few lines, and then sit down.

The process of lectio is a simple one. It is a form of prayer which can and should embrace every level of prayer. The book used for lectio, whatever it may be, is chosen as a means of hearing the Lord speak in human words. This, of course, means that the Bible is the lectio book par excellence. Yet any book with a general spiritual orientation is actually nothing other than a commentary on the Bible, and so is quite acceptable for lectio.

As I mentioned earlier, there are four levels of mental activity: information—a gathering of facts; knowledge—a classifying of those facts; understanding—an experience which those facts represent; and wisdom—a relating of that information, knowledge, and understanding to our ultimate goal, which is God. The reading of lectio divina is oriented towards wisdom. In it we attempt to see the facts of our lives, our value systems and our experiences precisely as they relate to and further our part in the building up of God's kingdom. We also open ourselves, in the books we read, to the experiences of others and to their particular wisdom, and seek to apply it in our own lives.

The most important element in lectio divina, however, is openness to the inspiration of the Holy Spirit. This is the reason for the ritual and prayer used at the beginning. We give the Spirit the opportunity to speak to us through the Bible and through significant spiritual literature. This is a time given over precisely for this purpose alone. It is not seen as an opportunity to study (to gain information and knowledge), or to reflect specifically on our past (to gain understanding), but mostly to open our hearts and minds to the suggestions of the Holy Spirit as a result of our reading (this is wisdom).

We do not open a book in lectio divina in order to finish it, but in order to hear what it is saying to us. Thus we read slowly, carefully, and attentively, often stopping to reflect on the meaning. Sometimes we read only one page in an hour, sometimes many. When we feel the grace to do so, we stop and pray according to the inspirations we may receive. I have often spent six months or more on one particular book selected for lectio, and have reread particularly inspiring books several times.

There are certain books in which the charisma of the author still resides in vibrant, living power. For me one such book is *The Cloud of Unknowing*. I have probably read this book during my lectio close to a hundred times! Each time I read it, it is a new book offering new insights, furthering my love for contemplative prayer. It becomes a means of getting in touch with a spiritual master whose name I may not know but whose soul I can touch as often as I take up his writings.

Let me share something which I teach my novices in terms of lectio divina and prayer. I have already stated that the Scriptures are the best sources for lectio. This stems from our understanding of the Church's teaching on inspiration. The Scriptures are inspired. Traditionally this word has had two meanings. In the first centuries of Christianity, the dominant meaning was that when the Scriptures were read and listened to, God spoke through them directly to the assembly or the individual.

Another meaning for inspiration has also been more or less prominent at different times in the history of the Church. It had to do with the authors of the various books in the Scriptures. Inspiration here meant that the Holy Spirit was in some way present to the author when he wrote his particular part of the Bible. Thus what was written was under the inspiration of the Holy Spirit and must be considered as the word of God. Much of the theological speculation regarding this notion of inspiration had to do with the manner in which the Spirit influenced the writer. Did the Spirit actually dictate the words? Did he influence the style of the author, or let him use his own personality to express divine truths? Was the author used mechanically, as we would use a pen or a typewriter, or did he have more or less complete freedom of expression, simply being guided by the Spirit so that he would not teach error?

It was Martin Luther who restored to the Church the more important and practical understanding of inspiration. This aspect refers to the presence of the Holy Spirit in the word of God inspiring the listeners to believe, understand, and take to heart the wisdom of God expressed in the Bible, especially when it is read in the assembly of God's people. This meaning of inspiration has never been totally absent. It is readily demonstrated through our liturgical practices.

Note carefully what happens at Mass when the Gospel is about to be read. The priest or deacon stands at the lectern and personally greets the people: "The Lord be with you." The people respond to him and to his greeting: "And also with you." But then something incredible happens. The priest announces: "A reading from the Holy Gospel according to St. Mark," and then he disappears. He, the minister, is no longer present. The congregation simply ignores him as it now responds to the Lord who speaks his own word. The people reply: "Glory be to you, O Lord!" God is present and speaking as the Gospel is read. The people acknowledge this again at the end by addressing, not the priest, but Christ: "Praise be to you, Lord Jesus Christ!"

The presence of God in the Scriptures when they are read is a real presence. It is as real as the presence of God in heaven, in the assembly gathered in his name, in the sacraments or in the Eucharist. They are all different modalities of God's presence, but they are all real.

This is one of the ways in which Jesus fulfills his extraordinary promise to be with us always, to the end of the world. It is also a fulfillment of his promise to send us the Holy Spirit to remind us of all the truths which he has taught us. This does not refer simply to a repetition of doctrines or divine principles as though they were things we had forgotten. It refers to inspiration—a breathing forth of the Holy Spirit that allows us to recognize the application of Jesus' teachings in our lives, how we should live them, understand them, and apply them to the concrete situations of our daily existence—once again, wisdom.

It is not necessary for us to await the gathering of the liturgical assembly to hear the Lord speak and to experience his inspiration. We can do this whenever we open the Scriptures in faith. Here are some suggested steps for an effective use of the Scriptures in lectio divina:

1) Build a church. Create for yourself a special environment in which you will recognize that you are doing something different, something special, something that will bring you into God's presence. This can be done by going into your bedroom, closing the door, and lighting a candle. It can be done simply by kneeling down in a private place, offering a brief prayer to be attentive to God's word, and then kissing the Bible and sitting down to listen.

2) Be aware that God has already spoken. You could not even begin this prayerful reading if God had not first summoned you to it by his grace. "No one can say Jesus is Lord unless he be given the power by the Holy Spirit." You are already into your prayer. God has called you and you have answered by going apart, taking your Bible, and starting your prayer. Now it is God's turn again.

3) Allow God now to speak through his Scriptures. Open the Bible to the Psalms or the Gospels. Read, listen to what God says for a verse or two until you wish to stop and respond. He is speaking to you.

4) Prayer is a dialogue. Speak to God. Ask him for an understanding of the text. Ask him how it applies to you. Listen again to what he says in your heart, the Scriptural texts, or both, and then respond again as you would in any conversation.

5) Decide beforehand how long you want to pray. Maybe ten or fifteen minutes is enough. When your time is up, thank God for his presence and his wisdom. Be prepared, when you can, to extend the conversation if you feel so inclined.

Prayer is a dialogue. It involves a give and take, a listening and a speaking. God speaks to us, we listen. We speak, God listens to us. It is really as simple as that. We must, however, realize that what God says to us is of extreme importance. We must give him the opportunity to speak and we must give ourselves the opportunity to listen.

Jesus is the Word. He is the Father's response (dialogue) to all of our needs. Through him the Father is always speaking in human accents the very fullness of what he is. He is saying everything from the fiat of creation to the bestowing of grace in all of its forms on humanity, to the very final Amen which announces the complete fullness of his kingdom.

> The Word dwelt with God, and what God was, the Word was. The Word then was with God at the beginning, and through him all things came to be. No single thing was created without him. All that came to be was alive with his life, and that life was the light of men.

Because God is Father, he is personal. His word is addressed to every single individual in a personal way, responding to every need in every situation. Do we need to praise God? Do we need comfort? Do we need to be rebuked, loved, reassured, chastised, instructed, pacified? God always speaks the word that we need to hear (not always what we want to hear).

Using the Scriptures is an important and helpful way to listen to God and hear just what he is saying to us. I like very much the questions in the front of the Gideon Bibles found in every motel, questions like: Are you sad? Read such and such a text. Are you happy? Are you guilty? Are you mourning? Are you confused? Read such and such a text. This is just what I am saying. God is already speaking the word which responds to your sorrow, pain, joy, confusion. Through the inspiration of the Scriptures, you need simply open the Bible to the text where God speaks to your problem or your present joys and listen to him.

This is what we do in lectio divina, when we enter into a dialogue with the Lord. All we have to do is to select a Scripture passage. It can actually be anyone at all. Some people like to open the Bible at random. Others prefer to select some verses with which they are familiar and which may address some present need. This is a very fine idea.

You can even make your own list of favorite texts in your own Bible so you can turn to them when you need to hear them. There are times when you need to hear God say: "Come to me, you who labor and are heavy burdened, and I will give you rest." There are also times when we need to hear him say: "Depart from me, you sinner," or, "I am the Lord, I show unfailing love, I do justice and right upon the earth."

How wonderful it is to be aware of the Trinitarian nature of our dialogue with God. The Father speaks to us in his Word, the Son, whom he sends forth into creation to reconcile all things to himself. This very Son then becomes our response to the Father, equal to him and worthy of him in every way. And it is through the mutual love between the Father and the Son that we are lifted up. It is the Holy Spirit who enables us to listen to the word and to be taken up and returned in faith, hope, and love to the Father.

Let me share with you one example of how I have experienced the Lord through this dialogical process. It is centered around the story of the woman at the well in John 4. Remember the background: because of the negative attitude of the Pharisees, Jesus and his disciples had left Jerusalem and were returning north to Galilee through the territory inhabited by the Samaritans, the traditional enemies of the Jews.

He had to pass through Samaria, and on his way came to a Samaritan town called Sychar, near the plot of ground which Jacob gave to his son Joseph, and the spring called Jacob's

Well. It was about noon, and Jesus, tired after his journey, sat down by the well.

Several years ago I visited this well of Jacob. I sat down on the low stone wall surrounding the well, took out my New Testament, and turned to John 4. Suddenly the walls of the ancient Greek Orthodox chapel built over the well dissolved in the shimmering dry Palestinian air. In the distance, I could see Jesus and his disciples approaching the well. They stopped a short way away, and I heard Jesus tell them to go into the town for provisions. Taking no notice of me, Jesus approached the well and sat down on the opposite wall.

Meanwhile, a Samaritan woman came to draw water. Jesus said to her, "Give me a drink" The Samaritan woman said, "What! You, a Jew, ask a drink of me, a Samaritan woman?"

I had noticed that there was no rope at the well to draw water. The woman had brought her own. I also felt very enervated by the dry, hot atmosphere and hoped for a refreshing drink myself. Neither took any notice of me, however. Then Jesus said something that caught my attention.

Jesus answered her, "If only you knew what God gives, and who it is that is asking you for a drink, you would have asked him, and he would have given you living water."

"Wow!" I thought, "What an opening! If only I can get in on this." I *knew* what he meant by "living water"—the Holy Spirit! The woman, however, did not know. She thought he spoke of the well-water. Jesus replied:

"Everyone who drinks this water will be thirsty again, but

whoever drinks the water that I shall give him will never suffer thirst any more. The water that I shall give him will be an inner spring always welling up for eternal life."

"Sir," said the woman, "give me that water, and then I shall not be thirsty, nor have to come all this way to draw."

The woman's response disgusted me. How could anyone be so ignorant, so unmindful of grace, so materialistic? I got angry. How could Jesus make such a promise to this crass, ignorant woman—one with five husbands and presently living in adultery—and ignore me, who was so parched with a divine thirst? They continued to speak without taking any notice of me. The woman, uncomfortable with the statement about her husbands, changed the subject. She introduced the age-old Jewish--Samaritan dispute about the proper place of worship, but Jesus was having none of that. Finally the woman said something worthwhile (I was still being ignored). She said:

"I know that the Messiah (that is, Christ) is coming. When he comes, he will tell us everything."

At this moment Jesus turned from her and looked directly at me from across the well. Then he said to me:

"I am he, I who am speaking to you now."

Then, for the first time, I knew what was meant by the inspiration of the Scriptures. I had never been ignored by Jesus. This whole scenario was acted out for my benefit. Jesus came for me. Jesus taught for me. Jesus suffered and died and rose for me. I am as privileged and as loved and as personal to him as was that woman, as were the disciples soon to return, as were those who sat at his feet for the Sermon on the Mount. And God has inspired the Scriptures, established the sacraments and founded the Church precisely so that I might be the beneficiary of all that Jesus says and does and is.

"I am he, I who am speaking to you now."

We are told then by St. John that Jesus went into the town where many came to believe in him because of the woman's testimony, and he stayed with them and taught them for two days.

Many more became believers because of what they heard from his own lips. They told the woman, "It is no longer because of what you said that we believe, for we have heard him ourselves; and we know that this is in truth the Savior of the world."

Read, listen to the Scriptures in a prayer of dialogue, and you will hear from his own lips. You will believe, not because of what others have told you, but because of what you have heard from him yourself.

CHAPTER EIGHT

PRODIGAL FATHER

ONE OF THE ISSUES THAT we must pay particular attention to in screening candidates for the monastery is the matter of responding to authority. Most often this comes down to the type of relationship the candidate has had with the father or father-figure in his life. It does not take very long before new monks begin to identify the novice master or, later on, the abbot, in this way. Everybody, in some way or other, eventually relates to authority figures in their lives, whether this be authority in government, in the military, or in job situations, as they relate to their father-figures.

When their father-relationship has been an unhealthy one because the father was too domineering, too weak, or too unloving, many difficult problems can arise. Unknowingly the young monk begins to respond to monastic authority in the same way he responds to family authority. We are even told that our concept of God is related to our concept of our own father. If your image of God is of a domineering, judgmental, severe authoritarian, then the chances are that your father was such a person. If, on the other hand, your idea of your father is of a weak, wishy-washy pushover, then you are apt to think of God along similar lines.

This is a situation that is capable of correction. One way is to deal with one's father-figure, living or dead, in a mature adult fashion and, with counsel, to recognize the childish residue of love, hate, fear, and other emotions that still influence one in such relationships. Another helpful thing is to learn to know God from the viewpoint of someone who has a perfect relationship with him both as an authority figure and as a father.

It is with problems like these that the practice of lectio divina can teach us wisdom. As we saw earlier, the New Testament is concerned primarily with establishing the new relationship between God and his people whereby they call him "Abba, Father."

Jesus tells us that no one knows the Father except the Son and those to whom the Son has revealed him. One of the places where Jesus has revealed the best picture of the Father is in the parable of the Prodigal Son. Indeed, many have claimed that it should be called the parable of the Prodigal Father. This parable is found in Luke's Gospel, chapter 15:

There was once a man who had two sons; and the younger said to his father, "Father, give me my share of the property." So he divided his estate between them.

The younger son's request was not too extraordinary, at least, in this sense: Jewish law required that he should inherit one-third of his father's estate. However, this would normally occur only at his father's death. Surely the father must have had some idea what the lad would do with his inheritance. So the extraordinary thing is that the father did as he was asked. He gave the young man his share. Let's call the younger son Jim, and the older son John.

Isn't this how God deals with us? He gives us freedom to deal with his generous gifts in any way we wish—even to squander them. Is he then too prodigal? He does this knowing that his divine love can and will bring good out of it. Yes, there is a risk; but love takes such risks.

A few days later the younger son turned the whole of his share into cash and left home for a distant country where he squandered it in reckless living.

Of course, this is what we expected, Jim took off, flew to Bermuda, got a suite in the best hotel, bought a new sports car, got an expensive girlfriend, and blew it all.

He had spent it all, when a severe famine fell upon that country and he began to feel the pinch. So he went and attached himself to one of the local landowners, who sent him on to his farm to mind the pigs, He would have been glad to fill his belly with the pods that the pigs were eating; and no one gave him anything.

This is even worse than it seems. As we know, Jews do not eat pig's flesh. Even to own a pig is considered an abomination. How much worse it would be, then, to be the servant of a pig. Jimmy had really hit bottom. But, as we are told by A.A., when you hit bottom, there is no place else to go but up.

Then he came to his senses and said, "How many of my father's paid servants have more food than they can eat, and here am I, starving to death!"

It took an experience like this for Jim to appreciate what he once had. When Jesus tells us that Jimmy came to his senses, he is also telling us that he had been out of his mind—leaving his father and squandering his fortune, believing that this would make him happy, were acts of insanity. But now we can see why the father allowed him to do all of this in the first place. It would bring Jimmy back, this time with real appreciation for what he had.

"I will set off and go to my father and say to him, 'Father, I have sinned against God and against you; I am no longer fit to be called your son; treat me as one of your paid servants.'"

Something truly beautiful is being said here, not about Jim but about the father. When the son had hit bottom and there was no place to go, his thoughts turned toward his father. Here is a solution, someone who would help him no matter what shape he was in or what he had done. He knew that his father loved him. Somehow, that love now reached out to him. It need not have been so. There are many sons who would rather die in their misery than turn to their fathers for help. Some would be too proud, others too ashamed, still others would feel that they would be rejected by their indifferent or judgmental parents. But this is not the case here.

> So he set out for his father's house. But while he was still a long way off his father saw him, and his heart went out to him. He ran to meet him, flung his arms round him, and kissed him.

What a beautiful picture! What an expression of God's love for us, coming from God himself. Do we need an image of God? Even he could not do better than this. I think that these verses are the most beautiful lines in all the Scriptures. The reason his father saw him "while he was still a long way off" was that the father was looking for him! Day after day he must have stood in the doorway of the farmhouse and looked up the lonely road stretching into the distance to search for the straggling figure of his wayward son returning home. And one day, there he was! Jesus uses a beautiful phrase here: "and his heart went out to him." The father's love outran his body. His exuberance knew no bounds as he ran, hugged him and kissed him.

> The son said, "Father, I have sinned against God and against you; I am no longer fit to be called your son." But the father said to his servants, "Quick! Fetch a robe, my best one, and put it on him; put a ring on his finger and shoes on his feet. Bring the fatted calf and kill it, and let us have a feast to celebrate the day. For this son of mine was dead and has come back to life; he was lost and is found." And the festivities began.

Now it was time for Jimmy to go through his little scenario. Notice, however, that his father did not allow Jimmy to finish it as he had planned. He was not even able to say the words, "Treat me as one of your servants." His father was too busy restoring the renegade to his position of son. Nothing was too good for him.

It would seem that the story could, and indeed should end here. However, we cannot speak of God, especially of God as Father, without somehow speaking of man. God never reveals himself without, at the same time, revealing something of ourselves to us. And so the story must continue.

> Now the elder son was out on the farm, and on his way back, as he approached the house, he heard music and dancing. He called one of the servants and asked what it meant. The servant told him, "Your brother has come home, and your father has killed the fatted calf because he has him back safe and sound." But he was angry and refused to go in.

We are intended to see the stark contrast in the attitudes of the father and the elder son. "He was angry and refused to go in." Some people feel a sympathy for Johnny. After all, if his brother is restored to his former position in the family it will mean a lesser inheritance for him. Yet, all the estate belonged to the father!

> His father came out and pleaded with him; but he retorted, "You know how I have slaved for you all these years. I never once disobeyed your orders; but you never gave me so much as a kid for a feast with my friends. But now that this son of yours turns up after running through your money with his women, you kill the fatted calf for him."

The father loved both of his sons. He did not send his wife to talk to Johnny, nor did he send a servant and order him to come to the festivities. Rather, he went out himself and pleaded with him. Then Johnny let him have it. Jealous, unloving and unforgiving, he could see what his father was doing for his brother only in terms of himself. It is important to note that John referred to Jimmy, not as "my brother" but as "this son of yours."

> "My boy," said the father, "you are always with me, and everything I have is yours. How could we help celebrating this happy day? Your brother here was dead and has come back to life, was lost and is found."

The father did not miss John's disowning of Jimmy by referring to him as "this son of yours" because he subtly corrects him, "your brother was dead. . . ." The father uses here the same words he had used previously when he himself had run out to greet and forgive his younger son. There is no doubt what he intends to convey to the elder son by this. He is telling Johnny that he should have done exactly the same thing. He should have been watching for his brother so that he could have seen him coming in the distance. He should have let his heart go out to him; he should have run to him, hugged him, kissed him, and ordered the fatted calf killed because this his brother was dead and had come back to life, was lost and is found. Here is a truly wonderful story from which we can learn the wisdom of how to be a father, a son, and a brother.

CHAPTER NINE

BEGINNING TO PRAY

THERE ARE FOUR ASPECTS OF prayer that have proven very helpful in my own life and in my experiences in spiritual direction. They are:

1) Prayer begins with God, not with us.
2) God does not need prayer, we do.
3) The listening element in prayer is usually the most important.

4) Perseverance in prayer can consist in simply starting over once again, today!

Certainly no one would be surprised at any of these rather obvious statements. Yet ignoring them is a common pitfall in our efforts at prayer. We seem to know them theoretically but ignore them in practice. A brief consideration of each will bring out the difficulties, and perhaps lead toward a solution. It may be worth noting that all four involve a working-through of some basic misconceptions about God and prayer.

Let's consider for a moment the first observation: Prayer begins with God, not with us. Grace is necessary before we can pray. The invitation has to come from God—what comes from us is the response. God says (in Isaiah 58:9), "Before you call upon me, I say to you, 'Here I am.' " St. Paul reminds us that no one can say, "Jesus is Lord" without the aid of the Holy Spirit.

However, the problem is that our actual concrete experience of prayer most often does not seem to bear this out. Frequently we approach prayer with nothing but a sense of duty to urge us on. At least it generally seems that God's invitation is not present. The definition of prayer found in the old Baltimore Catechism affirms this—giving, as it does, not a theologically precise definition but rather an experiential one. "Prayer is the lifting of the mind and heart to God. . . ." This is what we often seem to be doing, and frequently it is very difficult.

How much easier it is if we approach our prayer from a God-centered perspective, and become aware of our prayer as a response, not as a beginning. When we "begin to pray" or think we are beginning to pray, we should be explicitly aware that, whether we are emotionally conscious of it or not, God has initiated this prayer. The invitation has already come from him, the prayer has already begun; the grace is present, and all we have to do is respond. A concrete awareness of this is both important and personally very helpful. It can serve to do away with much of the feeling of aloneness, dryness, and even boredom that can often accompany our efforts at prayer. We would even do well to explicate this idea in the concrete, in some such words as these: "Lord, I know that you are here. I know that you have called me to this prayer (Rosary, Office, Mass, meditation, etc.) and that I could not now be speaking to you without your previous invitation and grace. I now wish to respond to your call and to lift my mind and heart to you."

The second aspect of prayer which I would like to reexamine is that God does not need prayer; we do. Again, we know this in theory, but our practice is something else. We often have the feeling that we are doing God a favor—even to the extent of making promises of prayer (Masses, rosaries, novenas) if God comes through for us. The image behind this attitude is, of course, a very childish but nonetheless a very persistent one: God sitting around just waiting to hear from us and even feeling neglected if he does not! Obviously God wants us to pray. This is because we need it; because, as St. Augustine says, our hearts are made for him, and cannot rest until they rest in him.

An explicit awareness of this aspect of prayer can be very helpful—even without going through the many reasons for which we do need it. Prayer is as necessary for our spiritual life as well-balanced meals and exercise are for our physical well-being. Without prayer we are incomplete, undernourished, debilitated people living half-lives, centered on that most common of falsehoods, i.e., that we are sufficient unto ourselves. We do not pray then for God's sake, but for our own.

The third aspect I would like to stress is the listening element in prayer. By and large this should be the most important element. I refer here to our listening to God, not vice versa. I would not minimize the importance of our being able to speak to God freely, but wish nonetheless to stress the idea of listening. We have all had our fill of such platitudes as, "God speaks in silence," but when it comes down to hearing precisely what he has to say, that is another matter. I do not wish to deny the place of silence in prayer or the very real truth contained in that statement. What I do wish to emphasize here is the value of some concrete way of listening to what God is saying. The process of lectio divina, outlined above, may prove helpful.

The final aspect to consider is perseverance in prayer. For some people this is not a problem. Daily habits of prayer, the ability (even sometimes the need) to follow faithfully some kind of personal schedule makes perseverance relatively simple for them. For many others, this is not so. They realize the value of prayer, acknowledge their need for it, and even admit a frequent awareness of God's invitation to pray, but still feel that their response is lukewarm, infrequent, and mediocre. Here is where perseverance in prayer can consist in simply starting over fresh each day.

To realize this we have to break through another misconception, namely, that of God as a judge with a scale—good on one side and evil on the other. Whichever is the heavier wins! If our perseverance outweighs our neglect, we have it made, or the opposite is true. This, of course, is bad theology. God does not judge us. He simply sees us where we are. He does not weigh the merits of our past life against the evil (how many tons of evil will an ounce of charity offset?). The truth is that if at any given time, God sees us responding to his grace to begin over again, we have it made. This is true with regard to temptations to sin, prayer, or any other aspect of the spiritual life. God looks at us and sees that we have been neglectful in prayer. But he also sees us with this attitude: "Lord, I have goofed again. My prayer life is a shambles. My resolutions at reform have been futile, but I am not giving up. I am starting once again (for the millionth time!) this very day (not tomorrow)." What God sees is not a failure, but his son or daughter, weak but filled with good intentions. Indeed, if we can look back on an entire lifetime of failures in prayer, each one followed by a new beginning, we will have a lifetime of metanoia: a successful Christian life.

CHAPTER TEN

JOHN AND MARY

PRAYER, AS WE HAVE SAID, is a dialogue. As such, it can also be defined as a relationship. This, indeed, is what it truly is—a relationship with God. But this man-to-God relationship is human. Obviously it is a graced relationship, but nonetheless it is still human. Let us take a concrete example of a human relationship and see how it helps us to understand our prayer-relationship with God.

At some social gathering, let's say a party, John meets Mary.

The hostess introduces them in this fashion: "John, I would like you to meet my good friend, Mary. Mary, I would like you to meet my cousin, John. John, you will be happy to know that Mary is also a rabid baseball fan!" The hostess walks away and leaves them together. Now, if John and Mary simply stand there awkwardly, staring at nothing and saying nothing, the relationship will end before it really begins. However, this is why the hostess, conscious of her role, has indicated their mutual interest in baseball, to provide them with enough background to pursue their acquaintanceship.

And so, with a very superficial, external beginning, John and Mary enter that level of human relationship that we shall call the level of acquaintance. It is not a deep relationship, and should they find it difficult to continue a conversation, the silence would be uncomfortable, and even embarrassing. Such personal things as deep aspirations, peak experiences, intimate feelings, or life goals are not shared at this level.

This is a human relationship, then, on the first level. The couple meet, introduced by a third party who gives them some mutual background, and they pursue the relationship from there (or let it die). Understanding that our prayer relationship is simply a human relationship with God, it too must have an acquaintance level. For most of us this began in early childhood when a third party, perhaps a parent, introduced us to God. "This is Jesus. He is God. He loves you and will answer your prayers." And so we began our first level of relationship with God (or did we let it die?). This level expressed itself mostly in the simple prayers requesting favors, or in memorized prayers said without any profound comprehension.

We have many relationships on this level, many acquaintances. The tragedy is that, for some, the relationship with God never develops beyond this level, and their prayer life is limited to periodic appeals for divine help in times of trouble.

Let us return to John and Mary. As a result of the small talk characteristic of their acquaintanceship, each begins to realize in the other certain qualities which make their relationship worth pursuing. Each desires to get to know the other better. In order to do this, they make a date, i.e., they make arrangements to get together, just the two of them, so they can share and become further acquainted with those attractive qualities they are beginning to recognize in each other.

Now, in their conversation, they reveal more and more of their personal feelings, experiences, ideas, and goals. Perhaps John tells Mary things about himself that he has never before revealed to anyone. Her response is more sympathetic than any he has ever found before. Sometimes this response is merely a comfortable, accepting silence. No longer is silence between them awkward and uncomfortable. It is no longer a negative thing, but as they get to know each other better and better, it becomes filled with one another. They have now entered, not into a new or different human relationship, but into a deeper, more intense one. We will call this deeper level of the relationship the level of friendship.

After we become acquainted with God in prayer, we begin to recognize that he has qualities worth pursuing. And so we do just what John and Mary did. We make a date with God. We go apart with him in order to learn more about him and also to reveal to him intimate personal reflections of our own. This is done in many, many different ways. We may attend some form of religious instruction where we learn to know God better. We may read and meditate and listen to the Scriptures where God personally reveals himself. We allow his truths to form our lives. We talk over with him our successes and failures and our new beginnings. We internalize his truths as we witness them in others or as we read the reflections of others about them. In other words, by reflection or discursive meditation, as we call it, we become accustomed to speaking with God on a personal level, revealing ourselves to him and, at the same time, learning about him from the truths of his revelation. Our acquaintance with God has deepened to the level of friendship.

It would be good here to emphasize one point. The friendship between John and Mary is going to endure only as long as, in some way or other, they continue to date. They must, even if it is only by phone calls or by letter, keep up contact with one another. We have all experienced the strangeness of an old friendship which, after years without contact, descends once again into the awkwardness of mere acquaintance.

And so it is with God. If we are to continue with him, we must persevere in our spiritual reading and reflective meditation. Friendships do not remain stable. Either they are cultivated and grow, or they lessen. God, by reason of the free, bountiful bestowal of his grace, is always actively encouraging a growth in our friendship with him. (Imagine! He finds qualities in us worth pursuing!) It remains for us to cooperate.

Let us look now at the third level of human relationship as we see it in John and Mary. As they continue to grow closer to one another, their relationship takes on physical overtones. They desire not only the intimacy of shared thoughts but also physical closeness. This is the time when they are hardly ever seen alone. Walking arm in arm, holding hands, and kissing all manifest themselves at this stage. This relationship, when it has been preceded by a genuine friendship, represents an authentic growth. This affective relationship may develop most completely into marriage, where the sharing of both personalities and bodies are allowed to find their fullest expression.

But how can this human relationship on the physical affective level express itself in our human prayer relationship with God? The spiritual masters have given us many descriptions of this level of prayer. Some even refer to it as "the honeymoon period" because of its brevity, its place early in the prayer relationship, and its emotional, affective elements. During this period, prayer often takes the form of intimate conversations with God, not infrequently accompanied by tears, profound sorrow for sins, and a lively joy at the realization of God's love and redemptive activity. This period (as well as the friendship level) may often be interspersed with periods of spiritual dryness as God leads us into a deeper, firmer relationship.

One of the most obvious forms of this affective prayer relationship with God is seen in the charismatic renewal. When someone is prayed over for the anointing of the Spirit, he is not infrequently "zapped," as it were. This is often accompanied by tears, intermingled with expressions of joy and a desire to express and share the abundant overflow of graces.

More often, perhaps, it is a quieter experience which serves to fill and inform the basic prayer structures presented by the Church for our worship. This affective level has a great deal to do with the effectiveness of our prayer. Thus, for example, a priest or a reader who is functioning in the liturgy is given a structure (readings, prayers, canon, etc.). The power in grace that this structure is able to communicate depends in great part (though not entirely) on the depth of the faith, love, and hope of the minister. Also on the part of the recipient, the level of his affective prayer relationship with God will determine to a great extent how much he will get out of the readings and prayers.

It must be kept in mind, however, that our affective prayer relationship with God is dependent on our friendship with him. If we do not remain faithful to our periodic "dates" with him—going apart with him for a while—then our affective prayer relationship, as well as our friendship, will degenerate into mere acquaintanceship.

Now for a final look at John and Mary. Picture them, if you will, after many years of a long, sometimes difficult, but still happy marriage. Their children are grown, married, and gone. John and Mary are back where they began—just the two of them sitting alone in the evening in their home. John is perhaps reading the sports page; Mary is knitting booties for a grandchild. Neither is speaking. Indeed, Mary knows by now just how John feels about everything under the sun. John is equally aware of Mary's thoughts. Yet there is a deep communion between them that does not require words. They are happy just to be in one another's presence. This is what we call the relationship of love. Verbal expressions, word and symbol, are no longer necessary or even adequate for John and Mary to communicate. Their deepest relationship is known, felt, and expressed by something much more complete than partial and inadequate attempts to verbalize it. Presence to one another, without words or external signs, can be the fullest expression of this human relationship of love.

And so it is with God. The fourth level of our prayer relationship with God is the relationship of love, or what we call contemplative prayer. It is a simple, quiet, peaceful abiding in his presence. One old man who spent hours daily in the church was asked by St. John Vianney what he did all that time. "I don't do anything," he replied. "I just look at him, and he looks at me." This is contemplative prayer.

It is a very natural, albeit graced thing, which is lived rather than taught. It is a quiet, loving gazing on the face of God with the eyes of the soul. God is recognized, often even felt to be present, by his touching of the soul. God is known now, not through the mediation of words or thoughts or things. These have been used in earlier stages and have served their purpose. God is seen now with and within the innermost center of the soul, not in light but in darkness, a darkness which is not the mere absence of light but the blinding effulgence of infinite light. He is heard now, not in words, but in the Word who cries "Abba, Father" in the Holy Spirit in a profound and full silence.

One other thing ought to be mentioned in regard to all of the levels of our prayer relationship with God. We must respond in accord with each level of relationship to the voice of God as he manifests his will in our lives. This involves a genuine attempt to make central in our lives the great commandment of love, a wholehearted and generous response to the guidance of his Church, a frequent and informed participation in the sacraments, and a continued effort to carry out the duties of our particular vocation in life. Eventually these things will themselves be seen as a part of our prayer relationship. The distinction between prayer and activity will become less and less significant, until everything we do becomes a response to and thus a part of our prayer life.

It is important to stress the normality of these relationships—both with others in our life and with God in our prayer. The progression from acquaintanceship to love is a natural one (and only because of this is it able to be a supernatural one: grace builds on nature). We are all called to love God and, as St. Bernard says, the measure of our love is to love without measure.

The precise manner, tradition, or school of spirituality which we use to develop and express this love will vary with each individual. There are many ladders of ascent to God. Each has to find his or her own way. Nonetheless, it remains true that in our day, the approach to God sometimes called centering prayer has proven helpful to many, either as an introduction to contemplative prayer or as a simple, systematic approach which clarifies and facilitates contemplation. Centering prayer does presuppose that we are ready for the love-relationship with God and that we have passed through the levels of acquaintanceship, friendship, and affective longing, and do feel, as *The Cloud of Unknowing* says, "every now and then a taste of contemplative love by way of the action of the Holy Spirit in the very center of their souls, exciting them to love."

CHAPTER ELEVEN

Contemplative Prayer

——◦—◦◦—◦——

Officially, at least, the monks of our community are contemplatives. We are said to belong to a contemplative order, but what does that mean? Part of the answer may be seen any morning in our darkened church from 4 to 5 A.M. The still figures of the white-clad monks can barely be made out scattered here and there throughout the church. Some are sitting on cushions on the floor, others more traditionally in the choir seats. Until the clock in the cloister chimes the half-hour, there is not a stir. But then the monks arise and begin a silent, ten-minute walking meditation, covering the full circuit of the church, until they once again reach their original seats. Again they take their preferred positions and resume their meditations.

But is this contemplation? Are the monks engaged in contemplative prayer? There is no way to answer that question on an individual basis except by asking each individual monk. Certainly they are taught the principles of contemplative prayer, and there is a certain presumption even before they entered the monastery that deep prayer was a part of their lives.

Perhaps there are better words to describe the monks or the monastic lifestyle. Some prefer "a contemplative attitude" to "contemplation." This extends contemplation from something done merely at assigned prayer-times to an attitude of listening to God that extends throughout the day. Still others feel that "a monastic lifestyle" is sufficient. At any rate, contemplative prayer is sometimes easier to experience than to describe.

In the First Book of Kings, chapters 18 and 19, we read the fascinating account of the prophet Elijah and Queen Jezebel. Jezebel was the wife of Ahaz, who had married her in spite of the prohibition forbidding Jews to marry Philistines. To make matters worse, when Jezebel came to assume the throne of Israel, she brought with her four hundred and fifty prophets of Baal and four hundred priests of the goddess Asherah.

Elijah was fed up with King Ahaz's fence-sitting. "If Yahweh is God, serve him," he declared, "if Baal, then follow him." Then he told Ahaz to summon all of Israel together with all of Jezebel's pagan priests and prophets to meet with him on Mt. Carmel. It was time for a showdown.

Elijah had two altars built and told the people to bring two bulls for sacrifice. The pagans were to prepare one bull and lay it on the wood without setting fire to it. Then they were to invoke Baal to cause a fire to consume their offering. Elijah would do likewise and call upon Yahweh. The one who answered by fire was to be recognized as God.

So from morning until noon the priests called upon Baal by name, "Baal, Baal, answer us." But there was no reply. They shouted louder and, as was their custom, danced with abandon around the altar. All afternoon they ranted and raved and gashed themselves with knives and spears until the hour of the evening sacrifice. Still there was no reply, no sound, no sign of awareness.

Elijah then prepared his bull, laid it upon the wood, and told the Jews to fill four jars with water and pour them over the animal and the wood. They did this three successive times, and the water ran over the altar and filled the trench Elijah had ordered to be dug around it. Then Elijah stepped forward and offered a simple prayer to Yahweh. Suddenly the fire of the Lord fell from out of the heavens and consumed the whole offering and the wood. It licked up the water in the trench and scorched the very stones of the altar and the earth on which it stood. When the people saw this they fell on their faces and cried, "Yahweh is God, Yahweh is God." At this point, Elijah ordered the people to seize the prophets of Baal, take them down to the Kishon and slaughter them there in the valley.

Ahaz rushed to his wife Jezebel and told her all that Elijah had done and how he had put all of her prophets to the sword. Enraged, Jezebel sent a messenger to Elijah. "May the gods curse me," she said, "if by this time tomorrow I have not taken your life as you took theirs." Elijah was afraid and fled for his life.

But his troubles had just begun. He got as far as Beersheba in Judea, where he despaired and asked the Lord to take his life. Instead, the Lord sent an angel to give him bread and water. He ate and drank and, nourished by this food, went on for forty days and forty nights until he reached Horeb, the mountain of God. Horeb is another name for Mt. Sinai. Elijah entered a cave and waited.

He was told to go and stand on the mountain before God, who would pass by. Suddenly a great and strong wind came rending the earth and shattering the very rocks before him. But the Lord was not in the wind. And after the wind there was an earthquake which made the mountain tremble and caused the stones to fall in an awesome landslide, but the Lord was not in the earthquake. And after the earthquake, fire, but the Lord was not in the fire. Then Elijah heard the sound of a gentle breeze, and when he heard it, he hid his face in his cloak and went out and stood at the mouth of his cave. Then a voice spoke to him.

Something very interesting is happening here. There is a deliberate contrast shown in the manner in which God spoke to Elijah and in the manner in which he had spoken to Moses and the people in the past. The author of the Book of Kings wants us to see Elijah in terms of the past, but with a difference.

During the time of their sojourn in the desert, the Jews had been a crass, ignorant people who could only be brought to God by fear and a display of his power. When the Lord promised to speak to them (Ex. 20), Moses was told to put barriers around the mountain. Any man or beast who so much as touched the edge of the mountain was to be stoned. And there were peals of thunder and flashes of lightning, dense clouds, and a loud blast of trumpets. The people waiting there at the foot of the mountain were terrified. The sound of the trumpets grew ever louder, and whenever Moses spoke, the Lord answered him in peals of thunder.

Note the similarities between the story of Moses and the story of Elijah. Moses and the people were fleeing persecution from a pagan ruler. Elijah was fleeing persecution from Jezebel. Moses wandered in the desert for forty years. Elijah wandered in the desert for forty days and forty nights. Moses and the people were fed by a miracle from God. Elijah was given food and drink by an angel. Both were told to go to Mt. Sinai, where God would meet and speak to them. But here the similarities end.

The contrast now is quite deliberate and is repeated in three different ways. God will no longer speak to his people through fear. He is explicitly said not to have been in the wind, the earthquake, or the fire. Rather now he is recognized in quiet, in the peaceful sound of a gentle breeze.

We can take this story one step further, to another mountain at another time. On Mt. Tabor we have the same cast. There were Elijah and Moses talking to Jesus. And suddenly there was a cloud and from the cloud the voice of God spoke. His command was a step further even than hearing him in the silence of Elijah. His command now is to accept Jesus as his beloved son and *listen to him*.

This is contemplative prayer, listening to God. Not only listening to God but also hearing him, and especially hearing him in silence, beyond words and without images. This is the task of the contemplative pray-er. Is it proper to say that it is the task of the monk? Let's look at the place of contemplative prayer in our culture.

There are many reasons for the decline in both the interest and the practice of contemplative prayer in our culture. Until recently, the U.S. was a frontier nation with little of the leisure time necessary for contemplation. The so-called Protestant ethic, which held that God rewards the hard-working with material prosperity, and the fact that the Church in America has been missionary-oriented and activistic, tended to minimize the attraction to contemplative prayer.

On the other hand, contrary factors have led to a reaction against the materialistic, superficial level of consciousness that has dominated Western culture and hence necessarily the Church in the West. Many people, especially the young, have questioned the super-materialism of the American consumer society. Not having had to engage in their parents' struggle for security and financial success, they are able to look critically at some of the values which have over-emphasized this success. And so, many of America's younger generations have begun to search for a deeper meaning for living and a deeper level of consciousness such as that involved in contemplative prayer. (Obviously, this search is not limited to the young.)

Answers, sometimes partial ones, sometimes wholly mistaken ones, have been sought and found, for example, in Eastern types of meditation, esoteric cults, even in drugs and alcohol. Forms of meditation, some of them authentic, some not so authentic, abound in our youth cultures. Gurus, Zen sitting, Yoga, and TM have outlasted the '70s, and all of them attempt to teach meditation techniques. Sometimes these techniques are taught as prayer. At other times they are specifically presented as a merely natural activity performed for merely natural ends. Almost all of them involve a wordless, thought-transcending process that may closely resemble contemplative prayer and may even become dispositive to it. But I think it is important for us to realize that we need look no further than our own Church to find an authentic, well-proven, simple and theologically sound approach to contemplative prayer.

As interest has been rekindled in the Church in general, contemplative prayer has leapt over the wall. No longer is it confined to convents of Poor Clares or Trappist monasteries. It is returning to common practice within the Church. Books, articles, tapes, retreats and workshops on centering prayer are becoming quite common. Abbot Butler, an expert on Western mysticism, refers to contemplative prayer as taught in *The Cloud of Unknowing* as a teachable form of contemplation. Not only, he says, is it apt for priests and religious, but for the man and woman in the street.

Many people, however, seek meditation techniques as ways of rushing into contemplative prayer without proper preliminaries. Although no given individual can be forced into the theoretical structure of prayer as taught by the spiritual masters of the Western (Christian) tradition, there is a generally valid and universally experienced process of stages of growth from lower forms of prayer to higher. Most of us, in some way or other, have to go through these growth stages.

The great master of contemplative prayer, the author of *The Cloud of Unknowing*, warns against a too-hasty or too superficial interest in the higher forms of prayer.

> I charge you with love's authority, if you give this book to someone else, warn them (as I warn you) to take the time to read it thoroughly. . . . I fear lest a person read only some parts and quickly fall into error. To avoid a blunder like this, I beg you and anyone else reading this book, for love's sake to do as I ask.
>
> As for worldly gossips, flatterers, the scrupulous, tale-bearers, busybodies, and the hypercritical, I would just as soon they never laid eyes on this book. I had no intention of writing for them and prefer that they do not meddle with it. This applies also to the merely curious, educated or not. They may be good people by the standard of the active life, but this book is not suited to their needs.

Then he goes on to describe those whom grace has prepared to grasp his message. These are people who, every now and then, taste something of contemplative love by way of the action of the Holy Spirit in the very center of their souls, exciting them to love. This ought to include every Christian, at some point in his or her life. That is to say, contemplative prayer, in some form or other, really is for everyone. Instead of speaking of the extraordinary grace of contemplative prayer (the beginnings of which, at least, we are here equating with centering prayer), we should speak of the extraordinary grace of prayer itself. Given this great miracle, contemplative prayer, as well as every other degree or intensity of prayer, ought to follow.

In his commentary on the Our Father, Origen, one of the earliest theologians of the Church, says that the most marvelous thing about this prayer is not any particular phrase included in it, but the very fact that we can say it at all. The extraordinary grace lies in our God-given ability to bridge the infinite gap between God and man and to converse with him face to face. Once we understand this, the place which contemplative prayer can and should have in our spiritual lives is no longer a problem.

Prayer differs from prayer, not in essence, but merely in its degree of intensity. Basically the simplest recitation of the Our Father in faith, hope, and love by any child is the same as the most profound communion with God of the greatest mystic in a silence beyond words. The difference can be found in degree or intensity, but not in the nature of prayer itself.

In any prayer, of whatever type or intensity, the one praying so enters into the triune life of God as to become one with the Holy Spirit as the fullest expression of the love of the Father for the Son and of the Son for the Father. He becomes, as it were, Holy Spirit; the prayer activity becomes the Trinitarian expression of God loving himself.

CHAPTER TWELVE

THE WORK OF LOVE

———◆———

HOW DO WE BEGIN TO practice contemplative prayer? *The Cloud of Unknowing* tells us. First, we have to know and love God. This means we should already have developed a basic prayer life that is much more than a simple asking for favors. And as *The Cloud* says in chapter 35, "If you seek contemplation you must cultivate study and reflection in prayer." Frequent meditative reading of the Scriptures, good spiritual reading habits, and the frequent practice of traditional meditation would answer this requirement. We would include here also reception of the sacraments. As *The Cloud* says in chapter 28:

> When should someone begin the contemplative work? Only when he has first cleansed his conscience of all particular sins in the sacrament of penance as prescribed by the Church. After confession, the source from which evil springs will still remain in his heart despite all his efforts, but eventually the work of love will heal them. And so a person should first cleanse his conscience in confession and, once having done this, he should without fear begin the work of contemplation.

From these practices one is usually led to what *The Cloud* calls a stirring of love, a simple, peaceful inner desire to love God in and for himself with no other motivation. When we experience this stirring, we are already on the threshold of contemplative prayer. Many, many people know this experience but would hesitate to think of themselves as contemplatives. The reason for this has already been mentioned. We have been accustomed to feel that this type of prayer is reserved for a few chosen souls, perhaps only for members of cloistered orders.

True enough, it is reserved for chosen souls, but not for merely a few, because we are, all of us, chosen souls. Once we have an experience of this stirring of love, all we need are a few simple instructions to enable us to begin contemplative prayer. The author of *The Cloud of Unknowing* says that there are people presently engaged in the active life who are being prepared by grace to grasp the message of his book. He is thinking of those who feel the mysterious activity of the Spirit in their inmost being, moving them to love. He does not say that they continually feel this stirring, as experienced contemplatives might, but every now and then, they taste something of contemplative love in the very heart of their being.

The instructions as found in *The Cloud of Unknowing* can be given in four very simple rules. The first rule he gives is to sit easily. We should be comfortable, so kneeling is not (as a general rule) the best position for disposing ourselves for contemplative prayer. We should be in a quiet place, of course, in a comfortable position, away from doorbells and telephones.

The second rule is to place ourselves in the presence of God by a simple, brief prayer in our own words. There is a popular Byzantine prayer given to me by a priest of that rite who only came to an understanding of its content when he learned meditation or contemplative prayer as found in *The Cloud*:

> Serene light, shining in the ground of my being,
> > draw me to yourself.
> Draw me past the snares of the senses,
> > out of the mazes of the mind.
> Free me from symbols, from words,
> > that I may discover the signified, the word unspoken
> > in the darkness that veils the ground of my being.

It is sufficient, of course, for one to make a prayer in his own words, placing before God what he is about to do.

The third rule is simply to love God. This is both difficult and easy. In a very real sense, if we have gotten as far as the third rule we are already engaged in loving God and this is what contemplative prayer is all about. At this point, however, we don't try to think about God. We don't meditate on his attributes, or ask him for favors, or call to mind theological doctrine.

> . . . in certain times and circumstances it may be helpful to
> dwell on some particular situation or activity; during this

work it is almost useless! Thinking and remembering are forms of spiritual understanding in which the eye of the spirit is opened and closed upon things somewhat as the eye of the marksman is on his target. But during this work of love, everything you dwell on becomes an obstacle to union with God. For there is no room for him if your mind is cluttered with these concerns (*The Cloud*, ch. 5).

And with all due reverence, he goes so far as to say that it is useless to think we can nourish our contemplation by considering God's attributes, his kindness or his majesty, or by thinking about Our Lady, the angels, the saints, or about the joys of heaven, marvelous as these are. This activity, he says, is no longer of any use to you.

Of course, it is laudable to reflect on God's kindness and to love and praise him for it. Yet it is far better to let your mind rest peacefully in the awareness of him in his naked existence and to praise and love him for what he is in himself. Perhaps the best thing we could do is simply call upon God with love, and this in the fewest possible words. In chapter 37, the author of *The Cloud* says that contemplatives seldom pray in words, and if they do, their words are few. A word of one syllable is more suited to the spiritual nature of this work than longer words. The word Christ himself used might be best for this: Abba, Father, or, as *The Cloud* suggests, simply the one-syllable word, God. So we simply, peacefully place ourselves in God's presence and allow the love we have for him to express itself quietly in our hearts. We need do nothing else. This is contemplative prayer.

This is what you do. Lift your heart up to the Lord with a peaceful stirring of love, desiring him for his own sake, and not for what he might give you! Focus all your attention and desire on him and let this be the only concern of your mind and heart. Do all you can to forget everything else, holding your thoughts and desires free from involvement with any of God's creatures, either in general or in particular (*The Cloud*, ch. 3).

Now it is true that we love God in serving others, but we should likewise love God in himself immediately and personally, and this is what we do in contemplative prayer.

If you find that this approach to contemplative prayer appeals to you (and keep in mind that there are many different approaches), then you should try it. You should try it daily, even twice daily, for 15 or 20 minutes each time. Allow God to draw you to himself even to the point where you find that you have, without knowing it, ceased to speak in your heart the words "Abba, Father," but have been lifted above symbols and words into the quiet stillness of God's presence in the very center of your being.

The fourth and final rule is to end your period of contemplation with a simple vocal prayer such as the Our Father, said very slowly and carefully. Take a full two or three minutes. This will help to bring you back to everyday consciousness. This is necessary because contemplation does tend to lift us out of ourselves.

Falling asleep in the context of contemplative prayer need not be a problem. *The Cloud* says that if you fall asleep during this work of love of God, you should thank God. By this is meant that sleep must have been needed at that time, and God gave it as a gift. We simply return to our prayer "Abba, Father," when we realize that we may have nodded off or given in to distraction.

In regard to distractions, *The Cloud* advises us that

... when distracting thoughts come, you should pretend that you do not even notice their presence or that they have come between you and your God. Look beyond them—look over their shoulder, as if you were looking for something else, and of course you are. For surely beyond them God is hidden in the dark cloud of unknowing. Do this, and you will soon be relieved of anxiety.

A bit later he goes on to tell us that there is another strategy we are welcome to try. When you feel utterly exhausted from fighting your thoughts, you say to yourself, "It's futile to fight with them any longer." Then lie down before them like a captive or a coward. When you do, you commend yourself to God in the midst of your enemies and you admit the radical weakness of your nature. He suggests that you remember this device particularly, for in employing it you place yourself completely in God's hands.

If you would like to know if this type of prayer is for you, let me conclude with the words of *The Cloud of Unknowing*, chapter 75, which discusses certain signs by which one can determine whether or not God is drawing him to contemplation. The author of *The Cloud* says:

First, let a man examine himself to see if he has done everything he can to purify his conscience of deliberate sin according to the precepts of the Church and the advice of his spiritual director. Once he is satisfied on this account, all is well, but to be even more certain, see if he is habitually more attracted to this simple contemplative prayer than to any other spiritual devotion. And then, if his conscience leaves him no peace in any exterior or interior work he does, unless he makes this secret little love based upon the cloud of unknowing his principal concern, it is a sign that God is calling him to this prayer.

And finally, remember this admonition. If you wish to continue growing, you must nourish in your heart the lively longing for God. Though this loving desire is certainly God's gift, it is up to you to nourish it.

CHAPTER THIRTEEN

THE MYSTICAL JOURNEY

———◆———

THE MYSTICS RANGE IN AGE from 25 to 52. There are eight of them and hitherto they have been school teachers, musicians, students, forest rangers, salesmen, and so on. None of them have been on the monastic journey for even two years, but it is my job to convince them that they are mystics. They are, of course, novices here at St. Benedict's Monastery, and I am the novice master. I am presently teaching several classes each week on the mystical journey. We are all on this journey and we are all called to be mystics, even though most of us are frightened by the name.

Mother Teresa of Calcutta was once asked, "How does it feel, Mother, to have everybody call you holy?" "It is perfectly all right for people to call me holy," she replied, "and they should call you holy also because you have no less an obligation than I have to be holy." As it is with the word "holy," so it is with the word "mystic." We have an obligation to be mystics. This has to mean, of course, that becoming mystics is within the reasonable realm of possibility for us. And it is.

It is difficult for most people to assimilate the word "mystic" to themselves because of the many connotations that it has. It evokes images of plaster saints in various stages of ecstatic rapture, miracles, levitations, bleeding hearts, extreme mortifications and penances, monastic austerities from the Middle Ages, esoteric autobiographies and glorious canonizations (usually after a lingering death from consumption).

The real meaning of the word, however, is very simple and does not include any of these ideas; it simply means immediacy. A mystic is one who seeks an immediate union with God without the interference or mediation of objects, images, doctrines, thoughts or ideas. It does not mean that one doesn't use images, doctrines, or ideas, but that one eventually is given a union with God so immediate that there is no room or place for them.

Some of the great mystics like St. Teresa of Avila and St. John of the Cross have had marvelous visions, transporting raptures, and all manner of miraculous activity. This is why such things have come to be associated with the name "mystic," but they are not necessary components of being a mystic or even common elements usually connected with it. It is only by dissociating such things from the idea of the mystical that we can be brought to accepting the idea in relation to ourselves without deception or undue pride. Unfortunately, some spiritual writers in the past have made the claim that the mystical state is an extraordinary one, reserved to a few select souls, and not available to the average Christian. Today, however, virtually nobody would support that claim. Indeed, due to extensive studies and personal experiences among Christians and monks of Eastern religions, the mystical experience is seen to be much more common than previously thought and by no means limited to any one religion.

The great Christian mystics and mystical theologians, from the first to the twentieth centuries, all seem to agree that there is some kind of consistent, observable process to be undergone in the mystical journey. There are, however, great difficulties in interpreting their accounts, simply because they are forced to use images, metaphors, and poetic devices to describe experiences that occur beyond the superficial level of our daily consciousness. While there are some images common to many of them, such as the union of marriage, the darkness caused by excessive light, the pursuit of the soul by God, the transformation caused by fire in a red-hot brand, and so on, there are also many unique images used by various writers, and they can be difficult to interpret. In trying to describe the indescribable, every image is imperfect, every metaphor limps, and so mystics are often accused of being vague, imprecise, and often heretical. Yet there is sufficient common ground in their accounts for us to draw out a discernable path to the mystical, immediate union with God.

Probably the most common description of the mystical journey is in terms of the purgative, illuminative, and unitive ways. This is a description which actually goes back to the earliest centuries of Christianity, but which was greatly embellished and enhanced as time went on by theologians and mystical writers, as each added on to these notions the fruits of his or her experiences and speculative thinking. Some have felt that this description represents an overly simplistic portrayal of an extremely complicated process. Others insist that its value lies precisely in its simplicity. All agree that, at best, it is only a generic, artificial alignment of experiences gleaned from many different mystical authors, and that at no time can it be rigidly applied to any given individual.

Perhaps the most important thing to be aware of in the use of these three classical degrees is that the transitions from one degree to another actually comprise the mystical journey and are much more important than the plateaus or the completed stages themselves. The passages from the purgative way to the illuminative and from the illuminative way to the unitive are the routes where most of us spend a substantial part of our lifetimes. In fact, it may even be said that we never spend time in any one degree or other but somehow have a foot, at all times, in at least two of them (maybe even all three!). Although the three degrees are presented as occurring in a chronological sequence, in the actual experience of a given individual this is not always the case.

Because of the renewed interest in mysticism in our day, there is emerging a psychology of mysticism, but it has a long way yet to go. Meanwhile the three classical degrees remain a handy tool for dealing with the subject.

I have two other favorite tools which I use to teach about the mystical journey and would like to mention. The first of these, as I have already made clear, is *The Cloud of Unknowing*. My second tool is the work of another English author, this one from the twentieth century. She was an Anglican by the name of Evelyn Underhill (1875–1941). Like the author of *The Cloud*, Underhill was concerned with what she called practical mysticism, i.e., mysticism for the man or woman in the street without the exotic or esoteric trappings.

Both agree that the first step along the mystical journey comes even before the purgative way. This is a conversion. It may be a sudden, traumatic, overwhelming experience or a gradual, quiet change of heart which happens over a relatively long period. In this conversion one begins to realize that union with God is both possible and worth pursuing. In a negative sense, one realizes that one has hitherto been pursuing the wind. This first step, according to *The Cloud*, may be taken by a simple confession of sins and a resolution to live henceforth according to the norms put forward by the Church. Having resolved then to pursue the goal of union with God and to accept whatever tasks this goal may demand, one can be said to enter into the first degree, the purgative way.

This way can be described as a determined effort to come to grips with the world around you as it actually is, rather than as you have hitherto mediated it through your personal grievances, prejudices, ignorance, and erroneous judgments. What is required here is a deliberate process of recollection that, if persevered in, will result in a self-simplification proceeding from humility, from a reasonable denial of self- or ego-building pursuits, and from love. The previous chapters on lectio divina and dialogical prayer illustrate one method of achieving this recollection.

If this work is persevered in faithfully (St. Teresa of Avila says that it may only take a year or even six months), some wonderful things will happen. First, you will get to know God better. Your acquaintanceship with him will develop into a real friendship as you reflect on his wonderful works in nature and in scriptural revelation. Second, you will perceive his presence in the changing world of which you are a part. You will be conscious of something (or better still, Someone) abiding and stable and true in the fragmented and illusory pieces of reality. You will begin to know the God of immanence as he abides in the changing patterns of his creation. Third, you will confront your personal ignorance and prejudices, as they are in themselves, not as a part of your self. You will begin to realize the world every minute, in the manner of saints and poets. Things which you perceive will speak to you of themselves as they truly are—good and perfect creatures of God. Even what you had hitherto looked upon as evil, such as suffering and death, will be seen in their proper perspective as manifestations of divine providence. Fourth, you will find your true self somehow centered in a place of proper focus. In regard to the changing world, of which you are also a part, you will be sitting in the center of a thousand-petalled lotus, as the Hindus say, able to observe the world objectively and truthfully.

This work will not be done without some pain. You will be striving to become an artist and you must pay the price. Self-simplification, ego-destruction for the sake of any art demands work, exercise, practice, and perseverance—whether the art be music, painting, dancing, acting, sports, or mysticism. Humility is a necessary condition of real love. You will be like someone who is changing his sport from tiddlywinks to football. New muscles have to be developed and trained, a whole new outlook must be achieved, a new goal striven for. Even if it does not demand the austerities of the cloister, says Underhill, it does call for at least the discipline of the golf course!

A good part of this experience, at least in the beginning, will be a great pleasure. God will draw you to himself by letting you "taste and see that the Lord is good," as the psalmist promises. However, because it is only natural for us to love the gifts (i.e., the consolations and spiritual pleasures of our "honeymoon period") and to begin to forget the Giver, God gradually withdraws the spiritual pleasures in order that he might call us to love him for himself.

Thus begins what John of the Cross calls the dark night of the senses, the purification needed to draw us from the purgative way into the way of illumination. Oddly enough, illumination begins with darkness. Prayer, which had once been a pleasure, becomes a chore. Consolations are few and far between. Brilliant insights into God's love and providence, once so abundant in your meditations, cease altogether. Your restless and bored mind begins to look elsewhere for interesting subject matter, jumping about from one insignificant distraction to another. You find it almost impossible to focus your attention or use your imagination to illuminate God's revelation of himself.

At this point, there may even be physical difficulties in the form of sickness or accidents. You may experience family problems, even the death of a loved one. Everything seems to conspire against you and your once-glorious progress on the mystical journey. Yet somehow there is hope. Although it usually does not present itself in a consoling form, you do realize that you still love God and still desire to seek him in prayer. But strive as you will, your prayer life seems to be nothing but a helpless groping in the darkness.

It is important, here, to have the help of a spiritual director, preferably someone who has himself gone through this experience and who can assure you that you have not gone astray. People who are unaware that these seemingly negative experiences are to be expected, and even to be desired if one is to progress on the spiritual journey, can be held for years in a kind of purposeless limbo, not wishing to abandon their quest for union with God, but at the same time not knowing how to advance. It is enormously helpful to be told, even if one does not actually experience the fact, that the darkness enveloping this stage of the journey is not the absence of light but the overwhelming and temporarily blinding presence of too much light. It is the result of the divine illumination drawing close to us in a blinding effulgence. Could we but see what that light illumines in our present state, we would not be able to grasp it from the point of view of what it would reveal of God, nor would we be able to abide it from the point of view of what it would reveal about ourselves vis-à-vis God!

When this point is reached, you are now ready for a significant change in prayer. You are ready to enter into the beginnings of contemplative prayer. This may happen gradually and naturally by itself, or it may be facilitated by such methods as I described earlier. There is a slowing down of words and images as prayer becomes more and more unreflective. Even spontaneous acts of faith, hope, and love, once so common, become less and less frequent. Often the passage of time occurs unnoticed, and one even wonders if one has been sleeping during times of prayer. Yet at the same time there is a vague awareness that one has been doing the right thing, and even a feeling, as *The Cloud* puts it, of a stirring of divine love quietly exciting the soul.

You are now having a direct experience of God. You taste and see that the Lord is sweet directly and without any mediation. As St. Bonaventure puts it, you are tasting food, not talking about it. Your prayer at this stage, as compared with previous experiences, is like two men who have never seen a kumquat. They have heard of this unusual fruit and are interested in it. One of them, being of an intellectual bent, goes to the library and looks up kumquat in the encyclopedia. He finds descriptions of it, pictures of it, accounts of its growth and reproduction. Then he goes to the biology section and discovers where it grows, how to grow it, what its nourishment content is, what diseases affect the kumquat crops. After this, he goes to the business sections of the library to find out the yearly value of the crops, the import duties and retail sales. Then he peruses cookbooks to examine in detail how the fruit can be used in different recipes. When he is finished, the first man knows all about kumquats.

The second man simply goes to the grocery store, seeks out the produce department, buys a kumquat and eats it. While, as we have said, the first man knows all about kumquats, the second man knows kumquats. Ideally we want both experiences. Discursive meditation (lectio divina) helps us to know about God, contemplative prayer helps us to know God.

This prayer is called by St. Teresa the prayer of simplicity or the prayer of quiet. It is called by *The Cloud* the work of love. It is generally considered to be the first beginnings of contemplative prayer. By some it is called active contemplation, because it seems to depend, to a great extent, upon the willing activity of the individual to pursue it. Indeed the contemplative can, through his diligent will and the control of his attention, often recapture the experience of this prayer of quiet. Yet it often remains a fleeting experience.

To enter into the third classical degree, the unitive way, another real change must take place in the manner in which one apprehends God. Up to this point, in the progress through the purgative and illuminative ways, an arduous self-discipline has had to be enforced and endured. This results in a gradual control of one's wandering thoughts and desires by means especially of a steady, frequent practice of discursive meditation. A humble, realistic, unselfish, and loving awareness of one's world begins to show itself. The illusions and fragmentary perceptions of reality give way to a deepening of one's perceptions and a significant step forward into the larger movement of life. This inner development has been characterized by a continuous effort of the will which grows steadily stronger in its ability to exercise its most significant faculty—the ability to love.

Having earlier achieved an awareness of the immanence of God in the flow of created things, and having then come to an awareness of his transcendence in the darkness beyond image and thought, another change must now occur. This new change will seem to begin without effort, but it will really be the result of the disciplines involved in the transitions from the purgative to the illuminative ways. Further discipline will be needed to persevere through greater or lesser periods of boredom and difficulties in prayer. Often at this point one has a feeling of personal loss. There is an awareness that much remains to be done, but one is totally ignorant as to what to do or how to do it.

Now the soul is truly immersed in a cloud of unknowing. There are no familiar landmarks. Silence and darkness seem to surround you even though you seem to realize more and more that this silence and darkness somehow contain and conceal the goal you seek. Yet you are perfectly helpless to do anything about it. You are about to enter into that state of passive suffering called by St. John of the Cross "the dark night of the soul." It is the most painful and yet the most necessary phase in the mystical journey to union with God. Your education in humility is about to be perfected and the purity of your love tested. The final remaining bits of self-love must be taken away, even the very desire for spiritual satisfaction through union with God. Love begins when nothing is expected in return. Here especially must the password of John of the Cross be heard: "Nothing! Nothing! Nothing!"

At this point, incredible temptations may arise. Thoughts and images hurl themselves at the soul on a level more intense than ever before, often taking the form of attractions to sin that have long been considered conquered. Thoughts of self-destruction and even a sort of conviction that God does not exist may assail you. Yet strangely enough the soul maintains an attitude of generosity and submission. It keeps a willing acceptance of anything that may happen, even failure and death. It models itself after Job, who said, "Yea, even if he slays me, yet I will trust him."

The attitude of the soul at this stage is aptly illustrated in the terms of a medieval Zen story. A father and his young son were out for a walk. They came upon a huge tree. Lifting the boy up to the lower branches, the father ordered him to climb higher. Somewhat fearful, but trustful, the lad obeyed. Looking down from his greater height, the young boy heard his father shout, "Go higher!" Still frightened, but still trustful, he climbed further. Surely his father would not tell him to do anything that would hurt him. Now the branches grew thinner and the tree began to sway dangerously.

Looking down at his father, now a small figure a great distance away, the boy heard him say, "Now jump!" Incredible as it seemed to him, the boy was still convinced that his father loved him and would not let him be harmed. So he jumped. He fell and hit the ground, and his body was smashed to pieces. Then his father bent over and took the boy by the hand. He arose, and hand in hand they walked away.

This is a perfect account of the crucifixion of Jesus. He loved, trusted, and obeyed the Father, not merely to the point of death but even through and beyond death. "Yea, though he slay me, yet I will trust in him." Death is necessary if there is to be a resurrection. "Unless the seed die, itself remains alone."

If one endures through these trials the result will be a rebirth into a new level of existence. A transformation will be brought about not by oneself but by God's action. What takes place now, as St. Teresa assures us, cannot be clearly described. The soul is filled with a conviction of its closeness to God that is so certain and strong it cannot for a moment be questioned. Yet the experience is obscured in such a way that it is really impossible to describe it with any clarity.

It is here that we find the different images and metaphors of the various mystics and mystical schools. They differ according to the ability, background, culture, and education of the individual mystic and even according to the intensity and ardor, purity, humility, and love of the individual soul.

However it may be described, the experiences are similar. There is, as Underhill expresses it, the infusion of a mighty energy. Its vitality is poured into the soul, resulting in an experience which all thoughts and images are inadequate to describe. A totally new kind of life is given by God for which the old existence has no words. God is no longer an idea, a notion, or a doctrine, but an experienced fact and, in the last analysis, the mystics fall back on the only thing which they can say as they urge others to follow along on their mystical journey: Taste and see!

CHAPTER FOURTEEN

ESCHATOLOGY, THE LAST THINGS

WHAT IS THE PRIMARY GOAL of the monastic life? In the past ten years, I have interviewed scores of potential vocations. Fifty years ago, if someone came to the monastery to save his soul or to do penance for his sins, he would have been accepted without question. Today, such motives are held in suspicion, not that they are necessarily wrong, but because there are higher motivations and more authentic expressions of them that are expected today. Monastic aspirations are now expressed more in terms of loving God and desiring to seek him to the exclusion of all else, or in terms of aspiring to a set of values to be pursued in a supportive community which gives witness to desiring and seeking those same values. The notion of becoming a monk because one desires heaven or fears hell is not totally absent, but it is not a dominant reason for life-choices.

People today are more man-centered than God-centered. This does not mean, as it may seem, that God takes second place to man. What it does mean is that God takes first place in man rather than over man. This is one of the basic assumptions of liberation theology, and it is becoming more and more an expression of the thought-patterns and motivational rationale of our young people. It is a direct result of our theological conclusions stemming from the doctrine of the Incarnation and the specific teachings of Jesus himself as expressed in the Gospels.

Where should the priority lie? What is more important, our service to one another during this life, or the successful achievement of the ultimate goal of our salvation, eternal life with God in heaven? The two questions are, in reality, one, and the answers to both of them need not be contradictory.

Theology, like every science, has many branches. Monasticism is very much concerned with that branch called eschatology. Literally, eschatology refers to the study of the last things, specifically: judgment, purgatory, heaven, and hell. Monks are supposed to be already living the heavenly life—not in any unrealistic sense, however. Monastic faith is supposed to be so strong that monks live as though the veil of faith were lifted and they find themselves constantly in God's presence. Likewise their hope is supposed to be so strong that, in a sense, they already have the fulfillment of God's presence.

This is why monastic vows are not sacraments. A sacrament is a sign. Monastic consecration is supposed to be the reality itself. In monastic poverty, monks own nothing specifically, but all that God has created is theirs. In monastic celibacy, monks do not have children or wives, but are "as angels in heaven." In monastic obedience, they find the will of God.

In the past few decades, a fascinating element of eschatology has come to the fore. Due in large part to the great scriptural work of Albert Schweitzer, we have realized since the beginning of this century the primary place of eschatology in the New Testament. Theological speculation, influenced by this principle, has come up with some rich and wide-ranging ideas. It has been called a rediscovery of the eschatological dimension of Christian revelation. If it affects revelation, it must have significant repercussions on Christian existence. Karl Barth refers to the objects of eschatology as the "ultimate realities" and claims that they are the first principles of everything. The liberation theologian Gustavo Gutierrez goes even further, stressing how the eschatological theme continues to grow in our understanding of God's message today. He calls eschatology the "driving force" of salvific history. For him, it is not just another branch of theology, but the very heart of living and the key to understanding Christian revelation.

To understand eschatology as referring only to the last things is not enough. Extra-historical events such as the end of the world, the Second Coming, and the Last Judgment are of great import to Christians and, indeed, to all humanity, whether they believe in them or not. However, these great mysteries must be seen not as some far-off eventualities known only through faith, but as powerful incentives, divine goals, and even cosmic energetic forces calling into being our present-day activities and influencing them in the form and direction of God's eternal plan.

All of our present-day events must be directed toward and worthy of "the new city of God coming down from heaven."

This driving impulsion towards the future is grace, bestowing meaning, value, and divine direction to the present. As

Gutierrez puts it, "the attraction of what is to come is the driving force of history. The action of Yahweh in history and his action at the end of history are inseparable" (*A Theology of Liberation*, NY: Orbis, 1973, p. 164). We can only understand the real meaning of God's interventions in salvation history and in our own lives when we see that history and those lives from their eschatological perspective.

The future influences the present. The eternal now of God interfaces our past, present, and future, and reveals to us a value and significance in our activity that far exceeds the limited visions of the most farseeing prophets. History can no longer be seen as a record of the past; it is, rather, a "thrust into the future."

Monastic life receives its hope and joy from the expectation that eschatology thrusts upon it. The future hope of the world, stemming from God's promises, incarnated in the divine Word and given living force in the activity of the Holy Spirit, has its roots in the present, giving meaning to our labors and calling forth joyous eschatological celebration.

God's ways are not our ways, yet it remains paradoxically true that the divine Word has leapt into our midst and gives us a share in his own divine life. Somehow the task we have received from Adam to carry on the work of caring for the earth is going to result, not in another tower of Babel, but in the heavenly Jerusalem. The life force motivating and informing this process from creation to New Creation is God himself manifested as the Pentecostal life-giving Spirit, living among us as the Spirit of Christ, the bond and soul of his Mystical Body, and concretely manifesting himself in every act of genuine love brought forth on this earth.

Through all of this, then, monastic spirituality is informed, inspired, and motivated. The liturgical expression of monastic eschatological hope is the night office, or, as it is more aptly called, Vigils. Arising hours before dawn, monastic communities await in silent prayer, meditative readings, and psalmody the coming of Christ as symbolized by the rising sun. In faith and hope, the eschatological coming of Christ "on the clouds and in glory" is anticipated and somehow grasped and realized on a daily basis. The future is thrust into the present.

CHAPTER FIFTEEN

ONE THING NECESSARY

———•◆•———

ONE OF THE MOST CHARMING books that I have read in many years is called *Tales of a Magic Monastery* (NY: Crossroad, 1981) written by Theophane the Monk, a member of our community. Fr. Theophane uses a method of teaching through stories, a practice that is found in many monastic traditions, whether eastern or western. In fact the earliest monastic tradition in the Catholic Church has handed down to us a wonderful collection of stories from the first monks of the Egyptian desert.

These stories are intended to offer a challenge by being obscure, entertaining, or provocative. Zen monastics from the early Middle Ages have also made collections of such stories called, in their tradition, koans. Fr. Theophane combines the best of the Eastern and Western traditions in the following story, "A Visit from the Buddha."

> Why did I visit the Magic Monastery? Well, I'm a monk myself, and the strangest thing happened in my monastery. We had a visit from the Buddha. We prepared for it, and gave him a very warm, though solemn welcome. He stayed overnight, but he slipped away very early in the morning. When the monks woke up, they found graffiti all over the cloister walls. Imagine! One word: TRIVIA, TRIVIA, TRIV-IA, all over the place.

Another story from the fourth-century Egyptian collection of monastic tales says the same thing in quite a different way.

> Abba Jerome had left his cell in the desert in order to attend the Saturday liturgy in honor of the Holy Mother of God. While he was away, a thief entered his cell and stole his Bible manuscript from its shelf by the window. Abba Jerome saw him running away as he returned. He entered his cell and saw that his great possession, the Bible, was gone. Immediately he went to his cabinet and took a small silver chalice, his only other valuable possession, and ran after the thief crying, "Brother, brother, you forgot this chalice."

Jesus said the same thing: "There is only one thing necessary." If only one thing is necessary, then all else is trivia, as the Buddha indicated and Abba Jerome demonstrated. A total all-embracing love of God is the one thing necessary, a love involving all our minds, our strength and our souls.

There was a popular argument among theologians in Jesus' day as to how briefly one could state the essence of the Jewish religion. One rabbi was told by a pagan that he would become a Jew if the rabbi could recite the teachings of Judaism while balancing on one foot. The rabbi stood on one foot and said, "Whatever it is that you do not wish done to you, do not do to another." Along these lines, when Jesus was asked which was the greatest commandment, he could not answer the question exactly as asked. There are two commandments which cannot be separated: love of God and love of neighbor. One cannot be done without the other. Indeed, if priorities must be given, love of neighbor is to be seen as more important. Throughout the ages, spiritual masters have always insisted that the only yardstick that can measure love of God is love of neighbor. Jesus even identified the two when he said, "Whatever you do to one of these, the least of my brethren, you do also unto me." Jesus spoke of eternal life and the service of one another in the same breath. He did, however, subordinate one to the other. He clearly told us that our chief concern has to be mutual service. Taking care of this world, as it were, automatically ensures eternal life. In the parable of the Last Judgment, Jesus spoke of the separation of men into two groups. The sheep, those who ministered to him in the poorest of the poor, will possess the kingdom. The goats, those who did not minister, will be thrown into eternal fire. Where are the priorities here? Is it possessing the kingdom and avoiding the fire? No! It is feeding the poor and clothing the naked. It is loving service of one another.

Notice that in the parable neither the sheep nor the goats recognized the Lord in their services or disservices. They both ask, "Lord, when did we see you hungry and feed you?" So the immediate motive of the good men was not to serve the Lord and thus to come to eternal life. It was to feed the hungry because they were hungry. Their concern stemmed from their love. No doubt it is acceptable to minister to the needy because the minister desires personal salvation, but as a primary motivation, it is imperfect and is far from representing the highest Christian ethic. Love is the priority.

Gustavo Gutierrez has given us a beautiful summary of the twofold process of the development of humanity as the temple of God. In his view, God is a God of communion with his creation, especially humanity. As he elaborates, the oldest and most enduring biblical promises have to do with the presence of God among his people.

> I shall dwell in the midst of the Israelites. I shall become their God and, by my dwelling among them, they will know that I am the Lord their God . . . (Ex. 29:45).

Early in his dealing with his people, God often revealed himself on a mountain. One of his oldest titles in the Old Testament is God of the Mountain. Sinai or Horeb was an especially chosen site. Yahweh was seen to be even closer when his presence was linked to the tabernacle or tent of the desert wandering. Here Moses consulted with God, but always outside the camp, where the tent was kept. A dwelling-place of Yahweh was also implied by the ark of the covenant. These three things, the ark, the tent, and the mountain, emphasized the mobility of the Lord's dwelling-place with his people. He shared in their historical movements.

It was only when the temple was built that Yahweh could be identified with any precise, permanent location. But when the wanderings were over, the entire land of Canaan, centralized in

Jerusalem, was designated as Yahweh's dwelling-place. He was, indeed, not to be found elsewhere. So the different traditions merged. The mountain became Mt. Zion, the ark and the tent became the Holy of Holies and the temple. Strangely enough, the idea of God dwelling in the heavens only came to its full strength, emphasizing as it did transcendence and universality, when the temple was built and the people had a fixed place for their encounters with Yahweh.

When the Jews observed the destruction of the temple by the Babylonians, they were driven to focus further on the idea of a heavenly abode. This took on the notion of God dwelling everywhere, especially in their exile in Babylon. It was around this time that the prophets spoke up so strongly against purely external worship. They insisted that Yahweh was more interested in "a contrite and humble spirit" than in offerings of bullocks and goats. The interior attitude became the important one. Henceforth God was to be looked for in the hearts of men and women:

> I will give you a new heart and put a new spirit within you;
> I will take the heart of stone from your body and give you a
> heart of flesh. I will put my spirit into you ... (Ez. 36:26f.).

This new emphasis was seen most perfectly when the Word became flesh. Now God would be worshipped neither in Jerusalem nor in Samaria, but in spirit and in truth. Jesus presents himself as the temple of God ("He was speaking of his own body," Jn. 2:19). And where he is, there is the Father. Christ is the temple of God, and the Christian community, the Body of Christ, are the living stones of that temple. Now see where God dwells!

> Surely you know that you are God's temple, where the Spirit
> of God dwells. Anyone who destroys God's temple will him-

self be destroyed by God, because the temple of God is holy; and you are that temple (1 Cor. 3:16).

As Gutierrez continues, God's presence, instead of being linked to a particular people, is now universalized, extended to all the peoples of the earth, as the prophets promised. In addition, his presence is internalized in the heart of human history in the life of every human being. Thus the visibility of God is no longer in holy places, or in the temple, or in a particular nation, but in every person. Since the Incarnation, the profane (the word means "outside the temple") no longer exists.

The manner in which God is present is what decides the ways in which we encounter him. When he was present in the temple, he was encountered through temple worship. Now that he is in each man and woman, says Gutierrez, we meet him in our loving commitment to the betterment of humanity collectively and individually.

The Old Testament leaves no doubt as to the close relationship which exists between God and our neighbor. Proverbs tells us that "a man who sneers at the poor insults his Maker" (17:5). To know and to love Yahweh meant to do justice to the poor.

Think of your father: he ate and drank, dealt justly and fairly, all went well with him. He dispensed justice to the lowly and poor; did not this show he knew me? says the Lord (Jer. 22:15–16).

Where the poor are not dealt with justly, the Lord is neither known nor served. This is true whether we speak of the masses of the poor and social justice or of individuals and personal charity. Jesus made very clear the signs of God's kingdom: the lame walk, the prisoners are freed, the blind see and the poor are given the good news. To sin is to refuse to love, and to refuse to love is death.

Here is the test by which we can make sure that we are in him: whoever claims to be dwelling in him, binds himself to live as Christ himself lived (1 Jn. 2:6).

Love for God *is* love for neighbor.

We love because he loved us first. But if a man says, "I love God," while hating his brother, he is a liar. If he does not love the brother whom he has seen, it cannot be that he loves God whom he has not seen. And indeed this command comes to us from Christ himself: that he who loves God must also love his brother (1 Jn. 4:19f.).

The one thing necessary, then, is love. All the rest is trivia if it is not love or if it does not lead to love. Our encounter with the Lord occurs in our encounters with one another.

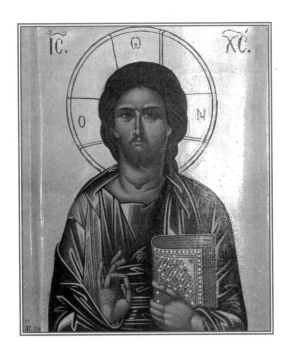

CHAPTER SIXTEEN

A Personal Christology

———◆———

I HAVE A SOMEWHAT FANCIFUL vision of what will happen
in heaven upon my death. After enduring whatever lethal
preliminaries are my destiny, I shall close my eyes and in an
instant (literally, the twinkling of an eye) open them again to
look upon the countenance of an old, familiar friend and gasp,
"Why, I know you!"

I hope that I shall see the face of Jesus, and I think that this
will be a face that I have seen thousands of times in this life; a

117

person whom I have served, prayed with and for, counselled, visited, clothed, fed, comforted, and buried. But even more significantly, I shall see a person who has counselled me, served me, clothed and fed me in the myriad forms of all his ministers on earth, recognized hitherto only in faith but now in knowledge and understanding. I shall know then even as I am known.

It is true that even now I do know and understand, albeit obscurely. My personal Christology, my answer to Jesus' question, "Who do you say that I am?" will be complete only in the event of my final salvation, but it is in process now. It will go on as long as I continue to reach out to grasp the victory he has won for me.

The Book of Revelation says that the Lord has a hidden name reserved for me that only he knows. Only he knows the true me, the real self that I shall become under his grace. But Jesus too has a hidden name, and it is my goal in life and death to discover it. This is my personal Christology: to experience, reflect upon and come to an understanding as to who this Jesus Christ is.

The tradition of the Jewish-Christian movement (the Old and New Testaments), as well as the ongoing and contemporary human experiences of people, are both intrinsic and determining elements in understanding God's revelation. God has revealed himself in the Scriptures, but our comprehension of this revelation depends heavily on the Church's experience of it and her subsequent pondering over it in her heart. Theologizing is an ongoing process following from ever-new experiences and needs facing the Church during her earthly pilgrimage. The Church is something more than the mere sum of her parts. In fact, each one of us is the Church. Any personal Christology partakes of and contributes to the Church's understanding of Christ.

We no longer see the Gospels as biographies of Jesus, but rather as interpretations. John sees Jesus as the pre-existing

Logos made flesh. Mark sees him as the fulfillment of the messianic prophecies of the Old Testament. Matthew sees him as the new Moses. Even a swift perusal of the titles given to Jesus in the Gospels reveal their varying interpretations: Son of David, Son of God, Lamb of God, and so on. Other Christologies are seen in the writings of St. Paul, in Hebrews, and in the Book of Revelation.

The last word about Jesus will not be said until the last man or woman on earth is asked to respond to the question, "Who do you say that I am?" Interpretive elements come from many sources, including the social sciences and the reactions of non-Christians. In the course of 2,000 years of living tradition, interpretive elements have accumulated continuously as Christians have attempted to express their experiences of grace in Christ.

Different interpretive elements can be seen at work in our own time. The Jesus of *Superstar* is different from the clown of *Godspell*; the Lord of Kazantzakis' *The Last Temptation of Christ* is hardly the harlequin of Harvey Cox. To think that any one image can exhaust the fullness of God's revelation in Christ is to belittle that revelation. Jesus came to us from the preexisting Word, a fact that first reduces us to awesome silence but then releases a riot of images. These metaphors touch upon the mystery of the Incarnation, but none of them can exhaust it. They are ways by which we look into the deepest meanings of life and explore the solutions that divine revelation offers us in Jesus.

There is a danger in all of this of attempting to recreate Jesus in our own image and likeness, of using Jesus as a propaganda tool to put forward our own point of view. For example, a Marxist portrayal of Jesus carrying a rifle is not authentic to the New Testament; such a distortion happens when a current ideology is grafted onto, instead of being confronted by, the Gospels.

How do we go about forming our own personal Christology?

There are a number of helpful questions we can ask ourselves. Certainly the first is to answer the question of Jesus—even write down our answer—"Who do you say that I am?"

The following suggestions may also be helpful. List ten adjectives that best describe for you the characteristics of Jesus as you have experienced him. Note especially the ones that come most readily to mind, i.e., the first three or four. Are they demanding or giving qualities? Do they serve to encourage your development as a fully human person?

Which of the many titles given in the New Testament is your favorite? Why? Which do you find the least attractive? Why? With what person, parable, or incident in the Gospels do you most readily identify? Why? What was Jesus' reaction to the same person or incident?

Write down two or three of the most significant conversion or grace-filled experiences you have had and relate them to Jesus as you presently understand him. Does your understanding of Jesus differ today from your understanding five or ten years ago? How? What is your understanding of the Church as the Body of Christ? To what extent does the rest of the world enter into this concept? How does this influence your practical daily activity, your reaction to the daily news, your prayer life?

What does it mean to you to say that Jesus is your personal savior? That he has won the victory for you? How does Jesus mediate the Father for you? Is your understanding of God different from what it might have been without Jesus? Do you see Jesus as a judge or as an understanding friend? (Do not answer the way you *want* to, but the way you actually do see him.)

Describe Jesus in writing in one page to a Jew who knows nothing of him, to a pagan, to a nominal Christian, to a devout Christian, to a child, to your father or mother. Does the fact of "the Jesus event" make any difference to you when confronting the problem of evil, especially of innocent suffering, or in your own personal suffering? What is the difference between Jesus and the Christ?

What saints or prophets, living or dead, best embody for you the reality of Jesus in their own lives? How? What three individuals whom you know personally best embody for you the spirit of Jesus? Is the Christ we worship today different from the Jesus you know from the Scriptures? Is the Jesus of liturgical worship different from the Jesus of your private prayer?

Formulate verbally or in writing a prayer to the Father in which you express your doubts or questions about the role of Jesus in your life. Conclude it with an expression of gratitude for the specific influences Jesus has had in your life. Let this prayer be as long as necessary, even extending over several days. It may be interesting to compare your answers with those of a close friend.

There are many Christologies. Anyone who has experienced in faith the Lord's saving grace, and has reflected upon this experience, has a Christology. The pondering is a necessary response to that grace. "Mary kept all these things in her heart, pondering over them." The more explicit we can make our own understanding of our graced experiences, the more effective they can be. Yet even this is part of an ongoing experience. The question, "Who do you say that I am?" is asked of us many times. Only by constantly answering it on a personal level will we be able to say one day, when the veil of faith is removed, "Why, I know you!"

CHAPTER SEVENTEEN

Fathers

THE INTRODUCTION TO MONASTIC FORMATION and
ongoing strides in monastic theology involve a close relationship
between present-day monks and the ancient monastic Fathers.
Their memory and teachings are preserved in collections of stories and sayings dating from the very beginning of the monastic
movement among the Desert Fathers of Egypt, Palestine, Syria
and the Middle East.

Our novices quickly become acquainted with such unique

and unusual names as Paphnutius the Buffalo, Moses the Black, John the Short and Anthony of the Desert. The simple, austere and isolated lives of these great monks of the third, fourth and fifth centuries echo down the centuries to fill the shelves of monastery libraries and enhance the hours of monastic lectio divina.

In the fourth century A.D. thousands of men abandoned the cities of the pagan world and fled to the austerity of the deserts of the Middle East to work out their salvation in lives of solitude, prayer and ascetic practices. Salvation through martyrdom, by shedding their blood as witnesses to Christ, was now becoming impossible. Nominal Christianity was socially acceptable as conversions from paganism become more and more popular among the higher class, even reaching to the exalted heights of the imperial courts. Ever since Constantine was converted by his vision of the cross with the words "In this sign, thou shall conquer" the cross was seen as a sign of temporal power. A world where political ambition was supported by conversion to Christianity reduced that conversion to a kind of slavish dependence on accepted, conventional values. This was something that could only be dealt with by a quick, complete and decisive flight from the cities of men, seen as thinly disguised centers of the kingdom of the devil.

Strangely enough these aspiring hermits fled the cities with their deceitful and confusing strongholds of churchly and political power, not to run from the devil, but to confront him. Standing alone in their sand-swept caves among the dunes of the forbidden deserts, these intrepid adventurers had every intention of confronting the devil where he really dwelt—in their own souls. This could only be done through prayer and penance. The long, lonely hours of vigils and the often-extreme ascetical practices of bodily mortification were intended to expose the wiles of the devil and to cast him out. Only thus could the open, honest, simplicity of exposure to God and union with his will be embraced in the contemplative attitude.

Solitude was seen as a way of stripping themselves from all the useless appendages of worldly fashions, whether pagan or Christian. These monks did not disdain the company of men in principle. They would often gather for liturgical celebrations on weekends. Their words of wisdom shared among themselves showed that their love of God of necessity embraced love for each other and, indeed, for all of humanity.

The direct simplicity of their stories wielded great power. One monk, John the Short, decided that he was living too close to others. He announced that he was going further out into the wilderness to live like the angels without the company of men. He soon found that he could not live even according to the standards of his previous monastic asceticism. He slept through his meditations, found fasting impossible and neglected his mortifications. Finally in defeat he returned to the loose settlement of hermitages and knocked on a door, "It is I, John the Short, returned from the desert," he announced. "Go away," came the reply. "You could not be John the Short, he has gone away to become an angel." Stories like this were not fictional but proceeded from lived experience.

These monks, whether they lived in absolute solitude, in relative communities called lauras, or in the teeming monasteries of Pachomius and Basil were well aware that they brought the devil with them in the form of a compulsive attachment to their false self systems. Only the trust would set them free. To know the truth about oneself was to practice the virtue of humility. Humility then was considered to be the foundation and the source of all the virtues. Abba Anthony is quoted as saying, "One day I was given to see all the deceits that the enemy has hidden all over the world. Lamenting, I cried out, what can get us through such snares? Then I heard a voice saying to me, 'Humility.' "

The fruit of humility was purity of heart. This was, as Thomas Merton says, "A clear, unobstructed vision of the true state of affairs, an intuitive grasp of one's own inner reality as anchored or rather lost in God through Christ." The Fathers never intended to give general, universal prescriptions but rather their words were simple answers to simple questions. They were answers always seen through the purifying access of experience.

In his book *The Wisdom of the Desert* Thomas Merton touches the heart of these spiritual giants when he writes:

> The Fathers were humble and silent men, and did not have much to say. They replied to questions in few words, to the point. Rather than given an abstract principle, they preferred to tell a concrete story. Their brevity is refreshing and rich in content. There is more light and satisfaction in these laconic sayings than in many a long ascetic treatise full of details about ascending from one degree to another in the spiritual life. These words of the Fathers are never theoretical in our modern sense of the world. They are never abstract. They deal with concrete things and with jobs to be done in the every day life of a fourth-century monk. But what is said serves just as well for a twentieth-century thinker. The basic realities of the interior life are these: faith, humility, charity, meekness, discretion, and self-denial. But not the least of the qualities of the "words of salvation" is their common sense.

Today, it is both the duty and the privilege of monks to introduce their novices to the rich and authentic traditions first expressed in the sayings and the tales of the Desert Fathers and lived out in the experiences of monks throughout the subsequent centuries. Today, with minds and hearts open through ecumenical dialogue, abbots and novice masters are just as likely to present to their young charges the wisdom and experiences of Indian Yogis, Zen Buddhist monks of China, and the Pueblo Indians of New Mexico.

PSALMS, THE PRAYER OF THE MONASTIC COMMUNITY

THE SCRIPTURES ARE THE MEDITATIONS and the prayers of the monk. From before the dawn and until the evening, here at 1012 Monastery Road, we assemble five times each day to listen to the Scriptures and to chant the Psalter, the Book of Psalms. In the Holy Rule, St. Benedict reminds his monks that the early fathers prayed the entire Psalter of 150 psalms each day, so they should be able to do the same, he chides them, at least once a week. He then admonishes his novices to memorize the Book of Psalms to facilitate their meditation and chanting.

The Psalms have always had a special place in the worship and devotion of God's people, both public, in the liturgy, and private, in personal prayer. It is the duty and the privilege of the monastic community to offer publicly the official liturgical worship of the church, and it is the duty and privilege of the individual monk to make this worship personal.

The Psalms for the monk are his prayer, his meditating, and expressions of his daily experiences. They embrace every aspect of his life. He discovers in them every emotion, every kind of trial and suffering and every attitude towards God, self and neighbor, from compassion to cursing, from desolation, sorrow and grief to thanksgiving, joy and elation. For the monk the Psalms are reproducible, personal, religious experiences embracing every aspect of his life. There is a psalm for him—and for each one of us—no matter where he is, how he feels, no matter what he has done or what has been done to him. His mind, emotions, deeds and instinctual responses all have counterparts in the Psalter.

As part of the sacred scripture, the Psalms are ultimately authored by the Holy Spirit in cooperation with dozens of singers, poets, musicians, soldiers, merchants, travelers, wise men and women, priests, prophets and kings. They are danced to and sung for birthdays, bountiful harvests and victory in war. They are lamented at funerals and contemplated in awesome wonder at a sunset or a violent storm.

The monk is called to make the Psalms his own. He is to allow that same Holy Spirit who inspired them to pray them anew in his own heart and life to call forth God's praise, to marvel at his awesome deeds, to beg his forgiveness and even to question his wisdom and providence.

From a scholarly point of view and based on research arising only in the twentieth century, commentators have radically changed their approach to the psalms. Previously they had used many different ways to classify them. They often tried to put them in categories heavily based on imagination of themes seen in their subject matter. Sometimes this was helpful, at other times not.

Psalms that described natural phenomena such as thunderstorms, starry nights, and arid deserts would be classed as nature psalms. Others, such as those that deplore past sins, were called penitential psalms. Relatively recent studies have shown that the psalms were actually written over a period of 1,800 years and were collected into one book, the Psalter, only a few centuries before Christ. They are classified now according to the occasions for which they were written. These occasions were almost always ritual or liturgical, such as temple ceremonies. Thus the royal psalms often were written and used repeatedly for coronation ceremonies. Others were composed to express thanks to God for favors such as recovery from illness, the birth of a son or a good harvest. We can use them both according to themes and according to the purposes for which they were written.

There is another approach to the Psalms coming from the practice of the earliest monks. They were used as subject matter for meditation. First, the monk listens to, recites or reads a psalm to understand its literal meaning. Why was it written? What did it mean to its author and its earlier singers? Then because the Psalms, like all of the Old Testament, were written to foretell of the coming of Christ, the psalm is read again to see how it could apply to Jesus, his birth, his life, death and resurrection and the final coming of his kingdom. Finally, the psalm is read a third time and is interpreted on the premise that whatever is said of Christ also applies to his followers. So the monk then applies the psalm to himself, to his community, to the Church in the modern world, all seen allegorically in terms of the chosen people moving under God's guidance into the kingdom he has prepared for them. These three ways of interpreting the Psalms are called the literal, Christological and moral interpretations. In some ways, often with differing emphasis, the monk keeps these things in mind, pondering over them as he chants the divine office. As he matures in his spiritual calling his understanding of the Psalms deepens and accompanies him not only day by day but also even over the years in his journey towards the fullness of God's kingdom.

INTERCONNECTEDNESS

———◆———

IT IS 4 A.M. ON A clear, cold winter morning. I am standing in front of the monastery watching the string of headlights wind its way along the mile-and-a-quarter length of dirt road stretching from the church to the county road just out of sight beyond the low rise of hills. Contrary to the usual silence of our peaceful valley, the underlying hum of the motors seems to call forth a sense of urgency. As I glance up toward the clear star-studded heavens, even these distant sparkling bodies seem to reflect some kind of cosmic anticipation, awaiting some earthly phenomenon of so great a magnitude that it will affect even their unspeakably distant destinies.

As the cars gradually begin to fill our parking lot, only the sounds of their slamming doors is heard as the occupants silently emerge and head for the monastery church. Most of them are carrying prayer benches, cushions, or blankets. They file past me with a nod or a quiet greeting, enter our reception room, turn left into the cloisters, and make their way into the fast-filling church. Only a few candles are flickering to break the darkness and lead the way down the atrium stairs while the light from our

Salve window casts its subdued colors upon the seated rows of people and the cushioned and blanketed floor space now filled from wall to wall.

It is now 4:30. Not a word is spoken, and no one arrives late to disturb the silence. Suddenly, a set of chimes is heard along the length of the cloisters and even that gradually ceases, seemingly absorbed by the pervasive stillness. The hour of meditation for peace in the world has begun.

The pray-ers have come from Aspen, Snowmass, and as far away as Glenwood Springs, some fifty miles to the west. There is a goodly sprinkling of very young and elderly people, but most of them are in their twenties and thirties. All have come in response to a worldwide plea. Someone had a theory that if forty million people could gather together at the same time throughout the world to meditate and pray for peace, a "critical mass" would be reached. I am not sure what a critical mass is, or even if the appropriate number was reached, but like many other churches and religious communities, we felt that our cooperation in this hour for peace was worthwhile. It was bound to have a good effect locally and even on a worldwide scale. It certainly fitted into the monastic approach to intercessory prayer, and the interconnectedness that exists among all of God's creation, within the Body of Christ, and in the communion of saints.

A brief but very significant prayer that the abbot recites on important occasions in the life of a monk (clothing, simple vows, monastic profession) requests that "the Lord will bring to perfect completion what he has begun in you this day." Herein is expressed the basic source, not only of the oneness of all humanity, but of the interconnectedness of all creation. That-which-is comes from God and is summoned by his infallible word to return to him with its purpose fully accomplished. "My word has gone forth from me and it will not return in vain" (Is. 55:11).

Philosophically speaking, one of the most fundamental principles of metaphysics is the statement *omne ens est unum*, i.e., all being is one. This being so, we do not have to search any further to understand interconnectedness. Not only are all men and women one, but they themselves are one with all creation, with all rational beings, with all sentient beings, with all vegetative beings, with all inanimate beings, and even with beings of other dimensions in God's creation. For many philosophical systems, and even for many religions, an experienced realization of this oneness is the goal of our existence and the cause of our immortality.

Yet if our oneness stems from the oneness of God, there is also plurality, in God and among his creatures. In Catholic doctrine, God is three as well as one, and in the mystery of the Trinity (tri-unity), his threeness is one and his oneness is three. We must expect this plurality as well as this oneness to be reflected in his creation, and especially in men and women who are made in his image and likeness. The unity in plurality among the human race and in all of God's creatures expresses itself in interconnectedness.

By God's grace and by his creative act, stemming from his very being, we have unity and plurality and interconnectedness. Among God's intelligent creatures, angels and men, the interconnectedness is most fully expressed when they are most fully in accord with God's grace. To be separated from God is to be separated from one another and even from inanimate creation. To lose unity or oneness with God is to lose interconnectedness—the result is isolation, separation, loneliness and, literally, excommunication.

When interconnectedness is lost, it can only be restored by re-union with God, by the very stuff, as it were, of God's being, i.e., by love. Radically, this restoration was accomplished for creation by our redemption in Christ.

Creation was made subject to futility, not of its own accord but by him who once subjected it; yet not without hope, because the world itself will be freed from its slavery to corruption and share in the glorious freedom of the children of God. Yes, we know that all creation groans and is in agony even until now (Romans 8:20 ff.).

The process of concretizing this radical redemption in Christ must focus on the heart of each individual, but not in loneliness or isolation. Interconnectedness with God is restored and "Christ Jesus, who died, or rather, was raised up, who is at the right hand of God, intercedes for us" (Romans 8:34).

And now we move into an understanding of interconnectedness as it is manifested in the doctrines of the communion of saints and the Body of Christ, and how monastic spirituality dwells at the heart of these doctrines. It would be helpful if we could see the idea of doctrine in a somewhat new light. It has been the nature of doctrine to define, to clarify, and to limit. Doctrines are based on tradition, a revelatory process used by God to communicate his divine wisdom. The earlier forms of tradition (e.g., the Scriptures) are non-doctrinal in their expression. Rather, they take the form of historical documents, tribal memory, letters, diaries, poetry, and so on. When the doctrinal content of this tradition needs clarification, usually as a reaction to suspect interpretations, the Church brings forth a doctrinal statement. This is usually an abstract statement, culturally expressed according to a prevailing philosophical thought category which clarifies (and necessarily limits) the matter under consideration. Some doctrinal statements come from very early in the Church's history. The Apostles' Creed originates from the first century. Some are very recent, e.g., the Mariological doctrines of the nineteenth and twentieth centuries.

It is not necessarily true, however, that doctrines must limit in order to clarify. They may, and occasionally have, been used to expand our understanding of God's salvific plan. A possible example of this might be the use that Leonardo Boff (and many others) makes of the doctrinal statement that "man" is made in the image and likeness of God (although even this statement is more poetical than doctrinal). The reference is to the emerging understanding of the feminine in God.

> Every indication exists that we are witnessing the emergence of one of the key archetypes of humanity's collective unconscious: the anima in all of its multiple manifestations. A like event occurs only once every several thousand years. And when it occurs, the axis of history suffers a universal shock, as men and women once more produce a new self-interpretation and redefine their interpersonal relations. Within the institutional framework of the powers that be, the image of God flashes forth with a new face (*The Maternal Face of God,* Harper and Row, 1987, pp. 2–3).

This general approach to doctrine—any doctrine—instead of being a limited, narrowing interpretation can expand to a broadening comprehension of God's dealing with his creation. Thus, the interconnectedness expressed by St. Paul in 1 Corinthians 12 on the spiritual gifts and the Mystical Body of Christ can be seen on a universal and even a cosmic scale extending far beyond its specific doctrinal limitations. It may indeed be the case that this interconnectedness, e.g., on a worldwide scale and beyond the commitment of baptism, is somehow distorted, minimized, or bent by original sin, but it is still there, and the image of the Trinity is still discernable, however darkly.

The doctrine of the communion of saints can also be seen as an intensified expression of universal connectedness, temporally as well as spatially. Obviously, there is a real influence stemming from the past into the present. However, through this doctrine, that influence can be seen as personal and ongoing rather than merely historical.

To some extent, the validity of the monastic experience can be focused in the context of this connectedness (I say "to some extent" because interconnectedness alone does not exhaust the meaning and value of monastic life). When St. Thérèse said, "One can save the world by stooping over to pick up a pin," she was speaking from a profound awareness of our interconnectedness. When monks and nuns go about the quiet, simple tasks and prayers of their days with a grace-filled awareness of the influence they have on all of God's creation, past, present, and future, they live out the doctrines of the Mystical Body, the communion of saints, and the reality of a universal interconnectedness.

I think that psychiatrist Gerald May expressed it most effectively when he wrote:

> Though political and economic conflicts may separate us and even make us adversaries; though we may not appreciate or understand each other; though our individual and societal attachments may cause us to harm and even kill one another, still we are irrevocably, irreversibly, together. This universal connectedness goes far deeper than ideas. It transcends even the concept that we are all children of God. For in the realm of contemplative quiet, beyond all ideas, beyond our rainbowed images of God and self, beyond belief, we share the same silence. We are rooted all together in the ground of consciousness that is God's gift to us all. We are all brought to life through that One Spirit that is unfathomable loving energy. In this field-beyond-image, our joining is absolute.
>
> There is nothing we can do to change it. When the Islamic mullah prays with true and quiet heart, I believe that

the souls of the Iowa farmer and the Welsh miner are touched. When the gong sounds in the Japanese monastery and the monks enter the timeless silence of Zazen, their quiet nourishes the hearts of the Brazilian Indian and the Manhattan executive. When Jews and Christians pray with true willingness, the Hindu scientist and the Russian police-man are enriched. Thus when you struggle with your own mind, seeking that quiet, open beyondness that may or may not be given, you do this as much for others as for yourself, and you are helped by the struggles of others in ways beyond all understanding. Even in the activities of daily life, any act of compassion, however small, somehow touches everyone if it is done with a true spirit of willingness, is like another drop of rain on a dry earth. It is well, I think, to keep this in mind (*Will and Spirit*, Harper and Row, 1982, p. 329).

And so we come full circle, returning to the monastery church filled with silent worshippers praying for world peace. The network spreads from church to church, from gathering to gathering over the world. And it spreads not only spatially to those praying specifically at that very moment, but temporally to those who prayed yesterday and who will pray tomorrow, and even to other dimensions of God's reality as the heavenly choirs unite with the earthly chorus praying to the Lord "for the peace and unity of your kingdom, where you live and reign for ever and ever."

RELATED TITLES FROM LANTERN BOOKS

THOMAS KEATING, THEOPHANE BOYD,
WILLIAM MENINGER, JOSEPH BOYLE
Sundays at the Magic Monastery
Homilies from the Trappists of St. Benedict's Monastery
144 PAGES, 1-59056-033-7

THOMAS KEATING
Fruits and Gifts of the Spirit
128 PAGES, 1-930051-21-2

THOMAS KEATING
St. Thérèse of Lisieux
A Transformation in Christ
96 PAGES, 1-930051-20-4

THOMAS KEATING, ET AL.
The Divine Indwelling
Centering Prayer and Its Development
112 PAGES, 1-930051-79-4

THOMAS KEATING
The Transformation of Suffering
Reflections on September 11 and the Wedding Feast at Cana in Galilee
64 PAGES, 1-59056-036-1

JEROEN WITKAM
The Eye Aware
Zen Lessons for Christians
176 PAGES, 1-930051-04-2

PIERRE RICHES
Faith, Hope, and Clarity
Catholic Faith in Today's World
176 PAGES, 1-930051-53-0

DANIEL LANAHAN, O.F.M.
When God Says No
The Mystery of Suffering and the Dynamics of Prayer
128 PAGES, 1-930051-90-5

JENS SOERING
The Way of the Prisoner
Breaking the Chains of Self through Centering Prayer and Centering Practice
352 PAGES, 1-59056-055-8

PAUL DAVID LAWSON
Old Wine in New Skins
Centering Prayer and Systems Theory
144 PAGES, 1-930051-29-8